Trial Of The World

Trial Of The World

Mubarak S. Almutawa

iUniverse, Inc.
New York Lincoln Shanghai

Trial Of The World

iUniverse, Inc.

For information address:
iUniverse, Inc.
2021 Pine Lake Road, Suite 100
Lincoln, NE 68512
www.iuniverse.com

ISBN: 0-595-32309-X (pbk)
ISBN: 0-595-66520-9 (cloth)

Printed in the United States of America

Contents

Preface

There must be a way of meeting the world's problems, of bringing reality to our calls for peace rather than the repeated official slogans extolling world peace!

There have been slogans all over the world that have misled us; our rulers have glorified these so-called peace slogans. But they are fakes. Used to impose power and authority, to justify the hoarding and deployment of lethal weapon. Leaders have used the phrase balance of power as an excuse for the accumulation of more weapons of destruction. Its seems not to occur to them to them that at any time their bluff may be called. A mistake during practice, an impulsive drive by one side against another in this frenzied search for profit, self-interest and domination.

All this has been done by the leader brought into this courtroom in the name of justice. We have deliberately sought the rule of justice in there case, for we would not subject them to the kind justice they have so often inflicted, without any consideration for the people's safety and security.

This has been our motive. We have jeopardized our lives for it. We mean no evil to those brought here. But we really believe that if things stood as they are much longer the world would eventually and inevitably explode in a nuclear holocaust. All the signs are there.

Mubarak S. Almutawa

1

Mary looked for one man, the man whose initial joined hers on the white handkerchief she held in her hand. The faces of the men lining the decks—the initial of her husband David and her self…

On the pier of one of the naval bases scattered along the Atlantic coast, Mary stood with a crowd of well wishers and the families of marines and their officers who lined the decks of the destroyers. Mary was waving farewell because the destroyer was about to sail with David, heading for a target pinpointed by High Command.

As she waved Mary tried to attract David's attention, clinging to those last moments before the ship heading out with its marines and crew. Round her, others too waved and grieving as the destroyer sailed away.

At last Mary stopped waving but her hand stayed extended as if to keep some contact with David-but knowing too that it could not be.

Marines officers David was assigned aboard the US Navy destroyer to a garrison mission in the Mediterranean waters of the Middle East. Mary have would dearly loved to have been by his side but of course it was impossible. Her duty was to stay at home and prepare for the birth of their child, the fruit of their marriage six months before.

Her hand still extended Mary stood still, surrendering herself to memories of the recent past. Then she wiped her wet eyes with the handkerchief, but it could not absorb her grief or eliminate the pain.

She turned and walked home with hesitant steps, taking her thoughts and sorrows with her. Her mind was filled with memories of childhood, her schooldays' friendship with David, the hours and days of fun she had shared with him later, when they would separate only when night came.

And still recollections flooded back, the wonderful reunion with David after years of separation when her family traveled and David joined the marines. At a distance they corresponded and never lost touch until one day they met by accident in an American city.

Surely it was destiny that planned it, that marvelous moment when their eyes met! More memories too, of the time when David came to her at her university and the hurt when they again parted.

Memories and the baby he had left inside her womb! A passing car had 'Just Married' in a large scrawl of shaving foam along its sides occupants were happy and singing. It reminded Mary of when she became David's wife and responsible for their home, when she knew the meaning of love and stability.

She could not find the will to go home. The sea beckoned-it had taken her husband away and Mary remembered how she and David had discussed the army and national duty.

'We all want stability and peace of mind!' he said. 'We feel for our homeland, loved by its soldiers as they do their wives!'

'But the love of a wife is an instinctive human thing,' insisted Mary. 'There can be no peace of mind in the love of military life is stronger than the love a soldier feels for his wife. Surely there is a huge difference between one's duty and one's wife!'

David shook his head. 'Yes, but is duty and to ensure a good life with you I have to defend our country.'

Mary was not convinced. She wanted more reassurance. 'Does everyone join their armed forces because that is a national duty and not for any other reason?'

He smiled at her innocence. It seemed her woman's instincts could not accept his own commitment. 'Duty, social of love of homeland-all of these may be the motive for becoming a soldier.'

You see,' she insisted, 'our homeland dominates the world. There is no need for all that continuous military training, those maneuvers in other countries. Defense of our country should be the job of military schools so that ordinary people could be free to enjoy their families and build their lives.'

David smiled again, trying to agree while disagreeing with Mary. You're saying all this because I'm your husband and you think the way I do. So you must accept that the national service is inevitable for everyone, regardless of their education…'

But Mary broke in, 'Duty to our homeland, yes. But what kind of duty? Does it mean we must give aid to nations we have no friendly connections with? Our men should defend our land, not another's!'

Holding his hand up, David said, 'what about out treaties pledging to defend our signatories? What about international friendship?'

His logic won the day; Mary could find no more arguments. It was obvious that the ordinary people had no choice. The leaders could give orders, which ignored any kind of humanitarianism.

David had not finished. 'The law and the power are indivisible. Power is essential for the enforcement of law and it applies to us all. Of course the law can make mistakes. And who pays for them but us?'

Mary tried another tack. 'It is a mistake when our leaders send our sons to defend a nation by destroying another, even if we had no real relations with either, other than a loyalty of some kind. Are we not using our power against innocent peoples because of some misguided humanity of ours? Why do we offer to interfere by using our army, when our leaders gain nothing from it?'

The argument went on, with David talking about leaders are only humans and they can make legal errors and mistakes. But leaders can cover up their faults by claiming that their actions are justified, leading to secret alliances. This gave them a lot of influence over smaller states.

It did not convince Mary. 'This is just the sort of oppression that we create-we convinced ourselves, wrongly I feel, that it is duty.'

Oppression? Well, you see supreme command always sees the matter a different way. They believe that power requires oppression. Where power prevails, weakness is crushed!'

It seemed that David felt he should support the leaders and Mary remembered how the argument had ended-with her shouting that the first to suffer, the people, are the oppressed.

She kept walking and walking, thinking to herself about oppression and how it had affected their lives. When she reached home she fell onto the bed and cried, as if she were drowning in a lake of tears, finally sleeping.

When she woke Make thought briefly that David was there, then the memory returned and she cried more. It was lunch time but Mary was not hungry, remembering now the year before her marriage, of the months of happiness. Would that they could return!

As the days past Mary could not lose the pangs of loneliness. She would sit and think, 'David sat there. He was hungry and tired and I would make him a sandwich. On that sofa we used to sit and cuddle, teasing me while I got a meal ready.'

And she remembered his quiet words as he spoke of his love. Beautiful dreams they were, dreams of planning their family, how they would fill the house with childish laughter.

Mary put her hand on the slowly growing swell of her belly. A tear ran down her cheek as she worried about the baby who might arrive without the comfortable presence of her husband. Who would be there to share her happiness? She rose to make a cup of tea and as she filled the kettle she looked out into the garden and cried again.

'David and I planted those flowers!' Now they had withered and died because David had not tended and watered them as he used to do every morning and evening.

Dead flowers with no fragrance.

She felt like those flowers, she too missed the care that they had died for a lack of. Self-pity took control of Mary. She felt that their love had vanished because of the aims of supreme command. A mother with her unborn baby waiting for the fathers return.

The front doorbell suddenly rang. Her heart thumping, Mary jumped up. Of course it couldn't be David-or could it? No, he had gone and would not return until the war was over. Putting on a brave smile, Mary opened the door.

'He wanted it urgently!' said a man holding a suit, not knowing David was aboard ship on his way to war. The suit had been ordered so that David could look smart when he took Mary to the doctor for a check-up.

She kept a fix smile while she paid the bill. Unwillingly, she took David's suit to the bedroom and hung it alongside his other clothes, sadly running her hand over them. She buried her face in his suits in her sorrow, kissing the material, remembering. The supreme command would not understand. Weeping was not a part of their plans. Tears were a sign of weakness.

Mary left the bedroom, going into the study. She picked up a photo album a flicked through it. David's face looked back, happy, smiling, carefree. She remembered again, recalling every scene, turning the leaves and seeing him again and again until her eyes could weep no more.

She tried to pull herself together-it was no use weeping and her unborn baby had to be considered. She owed to David, it was their future.

After so much weeping Mary knew she had to rest. Perhaps she would forget reality as she slept. But the bedroom was full of David's presence, his pyjamas, his things, his everyday needs. She clutched his pyjamas and sobbed into them, forced to sleep alone, while even prostitutes enjoyed the husbands of others.

When she went to bed she only remembered more. The evenings when he helped her mark her pupils' homework, their courting, their playful tumbles. He treated her as if he were the owner of the world and she the only princess of the palace. She was both lover and small child, it was a wonderful time.

Mary tried to escape from it all, to stop remembering. But it was impossible. David was part of the house, the furniture, the simple everyday things like getting up early for work. The lover cannot forget the beloved, memories cannot be removed. They are engraved on the heart.

The attempt to sleep with a fitful one for Mary. She tossed and turned, waking only to cry, then falling a shallow sleep again. Now she woke, terrified, hearing screaming.

The pillow had soaked the dew of her tears and was wet. The screaming went on and Mary switched on the light. It was midnight and the screaming was coming from her neighbour's house. She got out of bed and pulled on her dressing gown and ran out towards Margaret's.

The lights were on and Mary shouted through the open door, 'What's the matter?'

Like herself Margaret was expecting, and her second child was due at any time. That time had come and Mary offered to drive her to hospital. But Margaret's husband Bernard was a doctor and had been called from the hospital where he was on duty. The pains of delivery were building up and she held Margaret's hand as the waited for the ambulance.

How would I act, Mary wondered. Would I wake and scream for help, or bare the pain on my own? Oh, David, where are you? Is it more important to carry out navy duties and serve your country than to comfort and protect your wife and baby? The sound of a car pulling up outside interrupted her thoughts.

Bernard took Margaret in his arms and she was so pleased to see him she cried. He reassured her that all would be well, that he would supervise the delivery himself and stay with her. 'Be patient and don't be afraid,' he murmured as she was helped the ambulance.

Mary asked if she could go with them, perhaps she could help? But Bernard said no, surely she would be taking her class after the vacation break in the morning? She looked exhausted and needed some rest.

'Don't worry,' he said. 'I'll keep you informed of Margaret's condition.'

There was nothing to do but walk slowly back to her house, that empty house. She ran her hands over her belly, scared of facing the delivery of her baby without David's comforting presence. Would she be strong enough to have the baby on her own? As if she was both father and mother? And she decided that was what she would do. Deliver it and write to David telling him that his baby was at home waiting for him.

How would I tell the doctor? Should I say that the baby is fatherless, which is not true? That David is not here because he is gone to defend his country's allies? Perhaps the doctor will say David should be at his wife's side at this moment. Margaret is so lucky. The pain of the delivery would be forgotten if Bernard is there to share it.

David's absence was all Mary could think of. She went back home and stared at his photograph on the wall. And she screamed at it, 'Why David? Why you? Right from the beginning I said your military service would create trouble! How many times were our dates cancelled because the marines took you away? You have left me lonely but you are a hero. Few men are like you-a hero who is never bored by duty. Never affected by sentiment and emotion.'

Mary slept until dawn brought dull reality back. She must forget the past and concentrate on the new day. She had an appointment with the doctor and her holiday was over, so she had to get to her pupils at school.

She prepared some breakfast even though appetite was not there. But food was essential for her and the baby, the child, which David had deserted through his duty. The food tasted like medicine which she was forced to take. David should have been there to take her to the doctor and then on to school. But he was gone.

Putting on a pink maternity dress, which made her look pretty in spite of her exhaustion and red-rimmed eyes, she gathered the books she needed for the day's classes-a task which she should have done last night but had forgotten about.

She left home early with the textbooks for her class in her bag. As she drove through their neighbourhood, memories came of David laughing with her, saying good morning to friends and neighbours. Over there, the florist where he would buy flowers for her everyday. Why take David from me? Could no one else be sent? I need him as a plant needs sunlight.

Then she was in the school. She found a smile from somewhere to greet the friends and colleagues crowding round, pleased to see her after the holidays.

'How are you? Marriage has made you even more beautiful!'

'That child would be as good looking as it's parents,' said Catherine, her closest friend.

But Mary's face only showed sadness. Embarrassed she could not speak.

At their mid-morning break Catherine came up close and looked into Mary's drawn, tired face.

'Are you OK?'

Mary broke down then, burying her face against her friend's shoulder, tears falling uncontrollably.

'What is the matter, Mary?' Catherine was deeply worried. 'I've never seen you in such a state! What's wrong? Have you quarreled with David? I can't believe that.'

She held Mary away from her and shook her gently. 'For heaven's sake, Mary, answer me. We're friends. Sat at the same desk together in school. No we work in the same school.'

Then Mary screamed at the horrified Catherine, 'David is away serving his country and I want him at home with me. I would rather him be out of work. Any kind of work than being a marine officer!'

Catherine took Mary into a corner and made her sit down.

'Tell me about it. You have always said how much David loved the service. How proud it made you...even how smart he looked in his officer's uniform. But you also said you were jealous of his love for the service. Have you changed your mind about it at all?'

'He has left me alone carrying our first child. Gone to defend a country which ordinary people have no contact with.'

'It is his life and you knew that at any time he might be sent away to fight. He was angry when you asked him to leave the marines and become a teacher.'

'I know of three men who found reasons for not going on act of duty. David should have done the same when we married. How can he forget his home, his pregnant wife and go off to fight?'

Catherine didn't know what to say and let Mary unburden herself, seeing she was close to tears again.

'I don't want him to die. To leave me with his child. I feel like a stranger in my own home. I hate it for the memory it holds. Yes, I love him and his profession. But he won't give up his patriotism for the sake of his home and family. Will the state look after me instead? Will it comfort me when I am in labor and having David's child?'

With her arm around Mary, Catherine said, 'Take it easy. David will be back with you when your child is born I'm sure. Don't give way to grieve. Try to live as normal a life as you can.'

'How long? Days? Months? Years?'

'David is a proud man, you will not change his attitude and you must wait for him to return. Then the smile will come back to your face.'

'He'll be away as long as the war lasts.'

'Yes, I know,' murmured Catherine, cuddling her still unhappy friend. 'But lets have patience. We are mothers and our duty is to bring our children up properly. Here in the school you are doing a good job. Wait and have patience. He may well be home soon. No it's time for class. I love you. See you later.'

In her classroom Mary greeted her pupils again. They were obviously pleased to see her and wanted to continue settling into school in a relaxed mood of the first period. But Mary insisted that they get straight down to work.

'Right. Now our first lesson is about chemicals and the process of manufacturing explosives from them. And how they are used in war.'

As she presented her subject she couldn't get out of her mind what David might be facing ahead of him.

At the end of the lesson Mary asked one boy what he had learned and if it had been interesting.

'No,' he said flatly. 'It only concentrates on the means of suppression and terrorism. As if there is nothing but war. I am not interested in the subject. Who will build a reactor or make a bomb when we are old?'

Another pupil said, 'The only people who are interested are the leaders. Who want to manufacture new devices and weapons to destroy the world in the name of profit. But they also create huge loses of people, flatten cities and prevent peace!'

Mary liked what she heard and she encouraged them to say more. 'Which one of you would like to invent destructive weapons? Or be a soldier dying violently?'

'No! No!' Came from the class. 'We are peace-loving. We hear about the millions killed round the world, we don't like modern weapons.'

A boy called Richard shouted at Mary, 'My father has been sent abroad with other soldiers to defend a country I know nothing about. He left my mother crying and I heard her all night.'

'So why do we all stand by and just watch the destruction of the world? Are we guilty too if our leaders disagree, fighting each other with bombs and rockets? We should work together to establish peace. It should be the point of our life and the beginning of our freedom.'

A girl spoke up. 'How can we do it if we have no voice to cry "Peace!" War dominates the world. It seems to be the only war!'

Her friend said, 'But, Sarah, will our leaders listen to us if we call for peace?'

'But our leaders believe they have already established peace,' said a boy called Mark and he was answered by Edward.

'Their peace is providing comfortable living standards, social clubs, free education, plenty of recreation facilities, luxurious residential courtiers. In this way they think they have established peace…'

'…security, stability and order,' agreed Simon.

Mary called for quiet. 'This is the way the major powers think, but what do we think of them?'

Sarah stood up. 'I believe it is one of the methods used by powers to keep us silent. They keep us happy so that we will forget the troubles of the world.'

'So for this purpose,' Mary said slowly and clearly, testing their reaction, 'we should work together, adopt a joint attitude, reject the acts of destruction. We must demand our right to feel stable and secure and denounce war and devastation. No more war! No more killing! Nothing is impossible if we are unified and stand firm!'

The class roared its support.

Mary smiled. 'We must all think carefully about this and talk again tomorrow.' Then she smiled at Richard. 'We will try to get your father back and prove to the sons and daughters of the world that we can establish peace. We are not evil people but we are when we behave like them. We all love peace and freedom, don't we?'

And the class shouted 'Yes!'

Mary continued with the lesson until the period was over and she left the room knowing her pupils were aflame with the ideas she implanted in them. She suddenly felt a relief. Now she knew she was not alone in feeling resentment and indignation at the actions of the leaders and commanders. She was proud of her pupils and things they had said as they denounced the reactors and atomic bombs. It was not childishness. It was looking forward to security and peace.

When Mary left the school her face was proud, as if she had seized the world. Some of her smile had returned. She would not surrender to dreams and be captive to tears and painful memories. Nothing would stop her from restoring her rights, for David's absence hers but her child's as well.

She loved David and missed him but just lately it felt as if she no longer needed him, but this didn't seem to alarm her. He had left her alone with her duty, which she believed equaled his. She would have to cope with time and tears.

No she must think of the baby inside her, and she headed her car towards the clinic. It was not yet aware that it would be born into a world in which it needed the breast of its mother and the love of its father.

In the clinic, embarrassed, Mary sat alone-the only woman not waiting with her husband to see Dr Eric James. He was a childhood friend of David's but their ways had parted when Eric went to the School of Medicine.

'Hello, Mary. Where is David?' He said when the nurse showed Mary in. 'He promised to come with you. I hope all is well?'

For some reason Mary hesitated to explain David's absence.

'Is he too busy? Did you fight? No, I don't believe that. David has never loved anyone else!' His eyes showed his curiosity.

'Well, he loves someone else today,' Mary said. 'He went to his new lover-he calls it duty,' and Mary spat the word out.

'I still don't understand. Where is he?'

Mary at last found the words. 'He left America on a destroyer. It's heading to assist an Arab state and I don't know when I'll see him again. How could he leave me before we're married a year? If he is killed my child will be fatherless.'

Dr. James patted her arm. 'Mary, calm yourself. We are all with you and David will have been under a great deal of pressure. Don't you understand that he is forced to go by his duty? He had no alternative but to obey orders. Or go to prison and what would that have solved? You know what the service means to David. He obeys orders given to him-like any good soldier. That is the reality and we must accept and cope with it.'

Mary stared back at Eric. 'Even you talk about duty! I'm tired of it. Taking care of me is David's duty. Or don't I deserve the same attention? Instead I'm the victim of duty! The trouble overseas isn't ours. Many countries have bigger armies. Why should it be us?'

Eric shook his head. 'Where peace is threatened there will be international disputes.'

But Mary would not be deflected. 'We shouldn't intervene in the affairs of other countries or defend their sovereignty with our youth. What guilt has my child if David dies defending a land not ours. Where is the guilt of widows when their husbands fail to return? Rulers cannot bring the dead to life! We must change the course of the world and send the evil for trial.'

Eric tried to calm her but Mary went on. 'Is declaring a war a duty? Tell me! There is no answer. Ordinary people have no say. We cannot put forward our feelings, our viewpoints, to the supreme command. They never listen. They do what they do for the sovereignty of the state-for its progress, its booming economy. Commanders have the job of maintaining the super-power, not helping suffering peoples of the world. They pretend to prevent war and maintain peace, but still manufacture atomic weapons in the name of prevention of war.'

While the doctor made his examination Mary's thoughts still ran riot. When he had finished, Eric said, 'Mary, your health is seriously deteriorating. It is affecting your unborn child and you must rest and have plenty of good nourishment. David might have been sent away, but you must not neglect yourself or your baby will suffer.'

He stopped her from interrupting. 'From the start you knew that your pregnancy is of a celiocyesis type, a potential danger. But you insisted on becoming pregnant. Now five months, you must look after yourself unless you want the child to be stillborn.'

Mary shrugged her shoulders. 'How can I enjoy rest and good food? I am lost without David's support. How can I lie on a tear-stained pillow week after week, all alone?'

'Don't be so sentimental!' Eric took her hand. 'Control your thoughts and keep hold of your feelings. Concentrate on completing your pregnancy safely. You say you want to "change the course of the world and send the evil for trial"?'

He stopped Mary answering. 'How can you do all this if you don't care for your own health? Try to live as if David is here with you-you his greatest love. David's not wrong. He's doing his duty for his commanders who he respects. He would not have gone if he thought you wouldn't be able to cope without him. You are also a teacher, you have a duty towards your pupils. Don't neglect yourself and act like those leaders you despise. Be strong!'

Mary smiled. 'Thank you. Perhaps I can do my duty too!' She left the surgery with a prescription and vitamin pills. By now it was sunset and the sky beautiful.

The days passed swiftly and Mary had letters from David once a month. She read the newspapers and knew that he was helping to defend Israel. She also read of Arab strength and the bravery of the youth suicide squads. Constantly terrified by the news bulletins, Mary often had sleepless nights, dreading that David would be killed in Lebanon. She started to write letters to the battlefront commanders asking them to leave Lebanon and pull their troops out of action.

One day she received an encouraging reply from the Phalanx, David's battalion. It was meant to calm her down. She was not surprised about this-it was typical of commanders who wanted to prove their power, even though their casualty rate was very high. Since her letters to the commanders had no practical effect, Mary turned to her pupils. The new generation which would establish peace and teach the world to think of peoples' rights.

It was a dangerous business, but Mary was determined to use the new generation as a tool for peace, no mater what the price to herself. Her pupils were keen and happy, finding that her calm advice was wise.

Mary said to them, 'Do we lose our glory as a well-established nation if we renounce atomic weapons? This is the theme of today's lesson and I want to hear all your views!'

'No one is allowed to say anything to the manufacturers of these weapons. So they are continuously being made. We must work actively as a group to create peace. We are the only instruments, which will awaken our sleepy world and save it from star-wars disasters. Let us work together against war, against killing.'

Mary felt a new kind of peace of mind. No more tears now. She looked forward to each day, to her class for more discussions. More work towards peace .

2

When Mary woke the next morning it were as if she were to meet a much missed and eagerly awaited lover. She had her breakfast in bed, then dressed and searched out the books she needed for the "Theory of Nuclear Disarmament" prepared by Simon.

Her whole attitude had changed. Now she wanted to find the views of other countries, where previously she had had no interest in what they wanted. But David's posting had changed all that. She was going to struggle to establish what was right. Her aim to establish a comprehensive peace so that the whole world would benefit.

It was a momentous idea and as she walked to her car she held her case to her breast, as if it were her newborn baby. It seemed as if she were seeing the world from a new angle. Now, even though David was away, she was happy. The kind of happiness beyond words. For she was engaged in a race against time.

In fact time was short. At school she barely had time to say hello to her friends.

Catherine smiled. 'I can see you are happy today. You must have heard from David.'

'Well, yes I'm happy. But not because of a letter from David. I haven't heard from him for over a month and I don't know why.'

Catherine frowned. 'Then why are you so happy? It's such a change from the misery you have shown lately.'

'Well, I can't live a normal life. I can just about live with myself. But I can't wait for destiny to change things while I do nothing.'

'I don't know what you're talking about. I just don't understand. What kind of destiny? And what can you change? Anyway, have a good day!'

Catherine walked away to her classroom leaving Mary standing there for a moment until she too went briskly to meet her pupils.

After they had exchanged good mornings Mary asked Simon to present an abstract of his work. Then, although it was almost certainly outside the planned and official curriculum of the school, she asked the class if they had read the research on nuclear disarmament prepared by Simon.

'So how do we benefit from it?' Mary asked at their general assent.

Simon looked at his notes, then he looked up and said, 'from the viewpoint of the authors who advocate nuclear armament, they say that it is the peak of civilization and advanced thinking. The highest degree of decent life. There is the principle that to have the necessary authority means to be able to lead the world. How could we be the most powerful without being well armed and in a position to rule the world?'

'In their opinion, armament grants liberty to the great nations. Gives them the right to live their way of life. Gives their people liberty of movement. Because the world knows they are powerful.'

The class listened and Mary asked Simon if there were an opposing view.

Simon nodded. 'Yes. From the silent majority who oppose the armament theory. From the view that it can only bring war and destruction to the world. But people would be psychologically uncertain and in constant fear...while the superpowers are all striving to win the armament race. Nuclear weapons give the powers political weapons over lesser nations.

Simon stopped and looked at Mary. She nodded encouragement so he continued. 'The leaders tried to devoid themselves of all feelings of humanity and peace. So why do they try to make us follow them? We should appeal for freedom to act as we want. To repulse armament. And work to maintain peace and security. The leaders pretend to avoid wars. They call for disarmament and peace through their political speeches and press statements. But they secretly strive for war. And they make the profiteers rich.

'Why should armament be present while the people are at peace and enjoy stability?' Mary asked. Simon smiled. 'The powers want full control. So they must be able to suppress peace by arms. No one supports armaments, Mary. It is nothing more than a submission to higher authority. We should be able to dominate the world by peaceful means.'

All the students agreed with this. It seemed to Mary as if they were echoing a cry from all the people in the state, regardless of the consequences. She felt proud, as if an effort from her would spread to all the people.

It made her happy, even perhaps slightly hysterical. It was a relief from the latent hatred she felt against those who had taken David away.

'I will never give up the thought of your return,' she said to herself. 'I am doing my duty as you are yours. But mine is based on sound family life. While yours is imposed on you. You have no freedom of choice. You have to carry out orders as if you were a machine. I do it for the sake of mankind. Tomorrow I wile tell the world that we are powerful as well as human.'

She knew she would see David again; his uniform decorated with medals won by his bravery. Wearing no medals, she would carry the fruits of peace and victory among the peace-loving nations.

She was not alone on her particular battlefield. There were thousands. Her troops were the mass of people. All David had was his soldiers, forced to fight a war they had not started. Surely, his love of duty did not mean he had to except a task he blindly believed was right?

'I don't blame you, darling, for your fatal love of our country. But I seriously criticize you for excepting it's wrong views,' she thought.

She realised she had almost spoken aloud but the classroom was loud with the opinions of students.

She called out, 'Are u all against atomic armament-both from a psychological and a humanitarian viewpoint? This class was specially organized for the discussion of armament theory. You may all say want you think. So we can find out whether the supporters of the theory of armament are right or wrong.

For a moment the class fell silent. Then one boy, Stephen, whose father was a naval officer, said, 'Can I say something? I am neither pro-nor anti-armament, but I believe that the issue relates to me. I think that the state should have the right to establish a strong military force. It should defend us in the event of aggression, so that we can enjoy peace. The state cannot do it unless it is a power and respected by other nations'

Mary nodded and said, 'But how can we become a powerful and awe-inspiring state? When it is achieved by bloodshed, atomic bombs, rockets and launchings to kill and mutilate thousands of victims?'

Stephen shook his head. 'No, Mary. I don't support world destruction. The possession of atomic weapons doesn't mean that the state wants war. I feel that the possession of such weapons works for the preservation of international peace and security.'

'And how can this be done?' asked Mary. 'These weapons threaten peace!'

Stephen looked around the silent class, waiting for his answer. 'We have to have atomic weapons. And even join the armaments' race of ICBMs and rockets. But without any intention of fighting with them. They help maintain the protection of our rights and show that our aim as a super-power is to establish a durable peace for the good of mankind. That we are people who have no wish to participate in war. Our competency to manufacture state-of—the-art atomic weapons does not mean we will face the world with them.'

But Stephen felt he was in a minority after his long speech. The pupils were angry, standing up and shouting, asking how his argument could be true.

When Mary had established order again, Richard could be heard demanding, 'Do you appeal for peace? Has your father's naval profession forced you to speak his military point of view?'

Mary said that Stephen's views were logical and reasonable.

The pupils who had criticized them were astonished.

But the leaders of the state don't think as we do. They always have their own way in their wishes for control over oppressed people!'

'You see,' said Mary quietly. 'If it is true that the state can maintain peace with armaments, they would never send their troops to control poorer nations which do not have sophisticated weapons. We deserve to live in peace. No one wants to see their mother or father the victim of a bomb, or deformed through atomic fall-out. Who wants to live as a permanent cripple? No one!'

Another student rose. Mary stiffened-she knew Richard's father was abroad David's destroyer.

'My father left to go to war too, Stephen. You know the fear when your father is gone. Missed his touch. Have any of you waited hours outside school, then remembered he is not coming to meet you? What is it all for? We cannot say "No!" to armaments and orders of the state, because no one listens!'

Mary took up his appeal to his friends. 'Listen to me, Stephen. If war comes, what will happen to you and your family? Atomic war leaves the earth foul. Your body will be thrown with others in contaminated ground. Not buried in a proper grave, but you will have committed no crime. You have no voice to complain about atomic armament, you say! You must stand up and cry "No! No!" to suppression and destruction!'

The class rose again and started shouting for peace until Mary told them to stop and sit down.

'I am proud of your thoughts. But we have to act practically to remove this potential danger. We can do it only by mass action. Do you agree or not?'

Again the students got to their feet, their voices raised in support of peace.

'We are with you, Mary! We are against suppression and terrorism! We want peace, security. Put an end to destruction!'

The bell rang to end the period and Mary dismissed the class, telling them that the next day's debate would be further research on the issue as it affected their generation. She asked Richard to gather opinions and points of view to be discussed openly and frankly the next day.

Mary was preoccupied with what was happening. It had been her best-ever school day. She was beginning to realise that almost everyone rejected armament. The school and the research her students could make just a starting point. An initial step for achieving her objectives. Armament was a very serious matter that must be overcome and eradicated. And she had to save David from his fate by his own efforts.

She was beginning to understand that it was her destiny to do something for the dignity of mankind, however unattainable that seemed. She spent the late afternoon in the public library and went home laden with books. She concentrated on studying reference books on armaments, researching for the next day's debate. It was well after midnight before she finally slept.

The next morning Mary was eager to engage in the discussion with her students again but her first thoughts were for David and their unborn child. It must be like David-clever, tactful, warm and kindhearted-but not willing to obey orders blindly. Her child must rely on its own judgments and not follow others because they were older. She did not want to produce a child to leave it prone to the dangers of oppressive ideology. Mothers should have their babies in a world of peace.

Before going to school, Mary called on Margaret to see her after the birth of her baby. She stayed for a while, mixed emotions making her want to laugh and cry together, witnessing Margaret's new role of tender mother.

Margaret stared curiously at her when Mary said, 'There is no guilt in a newborn child. But its life can be affected by a state whose leaders act in for their personal betterment, pretending that it is all in "public interest". It is a lie, a joke.'

Margaret didn't reply but nestled her small bundle closer as Mary waved from the door.

She nearly collided with the postman on the step. He put Margaret and Bernard's post into their box and then handed Mary a letter.

'Save me going to your house! Anyway you'll be wanting to read it immediately-hope it says he's coming back soon.'

The postman was used to her waiting everyday for special letters and was glad that this time he wouldn't see that obvious pain on her face.

'Thank you, thank you!' Mary laughed and ran to her car, hugging the forces' envelope to her. It was her first letter from David since she had began the discussions with her students and she suddenly felt weak.

David wrote that he loved her and missed her terribly. That his soldiers were in an alert state, still stationed opposite the coast of Beirut, waiting for instructions to move forward. They expected fierce fighting.

But what did David have to do with all this? He should just perform his duty on his own land. Not somewhere else. Where was the gain?

It all made Mary feel as if she was in the deepest dungeon of some remote castle, but still determined to save the world. She entered her classroom ready to begin the discussion of research agreed the day before.

Greeting her pupils as usual and receiving their 'Good morning!' in return, Mary started her lecture by asking if they had prepared themselves. A student said yes, but it was a very sensitive topic and worthy of discussion.

'So what is a research today?' asked Mary.

'It is the danger of atomic armament on the next generation,' replied Sarah at once.

Mary asked her to define it precisely.

But Stephen interrupted. 'Atomic armament is the desire to display arms. To destroy other countries and turn them into satellite states under another's rule. This no doubt can lead to another world war and catastrophe to the whole planet. All there will be is proscription, poverty, orphans, death. Civilization will go. People will roam about looking for shelter. It will generate fear in all generations.'

Sarah held her hand up. 'Atomic bombardment will turn people against the world. They will blame the world for the loss of their parents. The state isn't concerned about how many people are killed or deformed, how many cities destroyed. It is merciless. Without sympathy for innocent people.'

Mary asked Sarah if she had any kind of solution but the girl had none. 'But I presume you would like peace to be fostered and maintained?'

'Yes,' said Sarah.

But before she could go on, her friend Karen suggested, 'Peace should be maintained by the possession of arms but without their use. Except in the case of aggression against us. But we don't need atomic weapons.'

Sarah challenged her. 'Can we keep peace and show no intention of attacking by other states?'

How can we foster peace among other states if we can't maintain it in our own country?' Simon said.

Avoiding the last part of Simon's question, Mary said that the state could foster peace by avoiding disorder among other populations and preventing them from possessing atomic weapons.

'We can't stop the state from what it wants to do!' protested Richard. 'The government is part of a super-power-we have atomic weapons. It supports freedom of speech but only hears the opinions it likes.'

Sarah agreed with him. 'We cannot affect the authorities. They don't have a sense of humanity. They only think of weapons and armaments.'

'Waiting and saying nothing merely indicates submission,' said Mary. 'Only unanimous action can put can put an end to atomic weapons. What has anyone else to say about their threats to you and your children's children?'

They laughed with pleasure at the thought of their future families, then listened seriously to Mark, who only spoke when he had something to say.

'The next will hate its existence and will be emotionally handicapped. There will be a lot of antisocial behavior. Killing, rape, theft-and it will all be the fault of the state.'

'We must do something!' It was Mary who broke in. 'We cannot remain idle. So how can we define the danger of atomic weapons on the world's economy?'

It was Sarah who thought she had worked out an answer.

'When countries prepare to develop atomic weapons, other nations become frightened. They feel they have put all their finances and resources to averting the threat. This means that there are no funds for building or buying ships. Their economy is concentrated on the production of weapons-with any left for any essential domestic needs. And of course no funds will be deposited with international banks in these countries because of the fear that the money will be frozen if war breaks out.'

Karen added, 'You have forgotten to mention that those countries will use good fertile land for testing their nuclear weapons. You can imagine the effect on agriculture and domestic animals!'

It was Stephen who thought that those affected countries would revert to imports to satisfy their needs and cover essential requirements. 'Will other countries help by exporting or not? And if not, what is the solution?'

Mary stood up. She said there was no solution except a declaration of war. But not the kind of war threatened by super-powers. The are more concerned with retaining power than taking care of the public.

'Therefore,' she continued, 'we must all work together to try to save mankind before everything is burnt by atomic radiation. A real hell on earth.'

The period was over and Mary told her pupils to prepare themselves for the final debate. With the consent of the students, she then went to receive the permission of the head for a further classroom discussion so they could complete the final chapter of the research project.

When she got home Mary had her housework to do, tidying and cleaning and opening the windows to allow some fresh air in. the house used to be full of fresh flowers when David was home, but now there were none.

Catherine was due for a meal, so Mary had to take extra care. Her mind was full of the debates in school. How could she achieve international peace and save people from the threat of nuclear war? Her students had convinced her that she could do it.

The doorbell rang and Catherine stood there smiling and they hugged. Her friend had to been to see Mary at home since David left. They had a lot to talk about but Mary did not raise the subject of atomic armament. She felt it was strictly confidential.

When it was time to leave, Catherine looked deep into Mary's eyes and advised her to take care of herself.

'I expect you're still distraught, Mary, missing David. I hope he comes back soon and you'll be happy again. See you tomorrow at school!'

Mary knew her pallor was not all exhaustion or physical unfitness. It was emptiness, the absence of her beloved David.

Before going to bed she read up the subjects which previously she had never been interested in-armaments and matters related to the projects she had set her pupils.

She read for long hours, thinking about her students' opinions and discussion. She felt exhausted but still had to force herself to plan the next day's debate.

At last Mary slept. She had never become used to being without David's comforting presence and her rest was fitful. She rose early, enjoying the rising sun on the garden. After a quick breakfast she left for school.

It seemed her class had taken over when she came in. they were all talking at once and Sarah announced, 'Today we have an important topic which I think we have understood as much as we can.'

'So what are we talking about then?' Mary asked.

'Funding requirements of atomic weapons on the one hand. And the needs of mankind for a peaceful life on the other,' said Stephen.

'But can both be done at the same time?' asked Mary.

Immediately Richard rose. 'No!' he said. 'The government can't manage to achieve fairly a balance between decent living conditions and atomic armaments. Most of the finances would go towards atomic weapons, not for the public.'

Sarah broke in. 'They steal from the public the right to a good life. At the same time it is generous towards the atomic scientists and the manufacturers. They have prestige and prosperity while others not involved in anything to do with military things get very little. This imbalance creates a chasm between the makers of weapons and those who faithfully serve their country in other ways.'

Karen wanted to know why the government couldn't manage to achieve a decent life for all. Not through military strength but peacefully.

Mary smiled. 'You will never change your ideals, dear! I have already explained that there can never be true peace alongside arms.'

Not satisfied with this, Karen said, 'Why not let the government produce atomic weapons and make their money. Then it could be properly spent for the sake of the people, providing them with the means for a good life.'

'Yes,' agreed Mark. 'So there could be a balance between arms and living standards.'

'I believe,' said Mary, 'in the simple thinking and the faith that exists among us ordinary people. We differ for heads of state who are busy sustaining the arms race-not only for profit. But also for controlling and a show of power, even at the expense of mankind. States monopolise everything to hold their power-thinkers, scientists, innovators, capital funds and all the modern technology.'

Karen was still not convinced. 'I don't know, Mary. Every time I talk about the good faith of our government, someone tells me I'm wrong.'

'That is because our government rules as a super-power and we are all becoming well aware of its objectives now.'

'But the government gives us entertainment centres, sports clubs, playgrounds, stadiums, schools, cinemas, theatres and modern hospitals. This tells me that it does think of providing the people with good comfortable lives.'

Mary knew there was still a long way to go.

3

One day, while Mary was at school as usual, she received a letter assigning her to accompany a group of students on a visit to a nuclear reactor plant. They were to see the work going on there and the progress that the state had made, which would reflect its position in the eye of other nations.

It was her own class which had been chosen. At first, Mary accepted the visit like any other school task but deep inside she was very angry, even disgusted by the whole idea. It seemed to Mary that a visit would be a contradiction between going to the plant and the principle she believed in and told her pupils about. Nevertheless, she felt obliged to stay with the situation and during the visit discuss the scientific and technological advances made by the state.

Reluctantly, Mary read about the nuclear reactor and learned more about it than she had known before.

She told her pupils about the preparations for the visit and asked them to read up all they could about the technology and the explosive power of the nuclear missiles.

Some of the students rejected the whole idea and Mary had to tell them that it was their duty and that they had to go. But deep inside, she felt dissatisfied. It reminded her too much of her husbands attitude. What was he doing at this moment in a desert near the Gulf coast, thousands of miles away in the Middle East, except in the call of duty? Was he convinced in the role he was performing? It was his duty and he had to do it, he said.

Did he do it for the few dollars a month he was paid and because the money would secure him a good living? Whether he accepted or not was of no importance. Mary was confused and hoped that the visit would be for some reason cancelled. She told the children of her hopes but they seemed to want to go, they wanted to see for themselves the things they had been discussing theoretically. They thought that they would be able to talk to the people there and it might change their views.

It was a simple and innocent opinion. During the class discussions about their researches many of the students had rejected the idea of nuclear reactors and thus hoped to stop the manufacture of destructive missiles. The students wanted to go so they could put their views to put the people working at the reactor.

As time passed, the students the students read the subject up as far as they could. Then the day came and they were ready to go, keen to see this thing which had kept their thoughts busy for many months.

Like all students, some had no feelings one way or the other. They were joking amongst themselves and enjoying the trip. Others were deep in their own thoughts, some were silent.

As the bus made its way along the road towards the reactor plant, police cars passed them, hurrying towards it plant, their sirens wailing. Other cars were also racing along, all going to the large complex. It looked as if something serious was happening. The base was surrounded by high walls and each entrance had a strict security guard. Outside the large, main entrance was a huge mass of people, with police blocking the gates, stopping everyone.

Their bus approached the gates and stopped and the children tried to leave the vehicle, but Mary said, 'Stay here while I try to find out what is happening!'

She saw that many of the crowds outside were carrying boards with slogans against nuclear war. Some tried to get through the gates, some even put ladders against the walls and tried to get in that way. But the police stood firm and were asking for reinforcements.

Mary admired the protesters and knew that if she were not on duty as a teacher she would join the protest. Some of her pupils had got off the bus and were joining the crowds, asking them what they were doing there. Other children just sat and watched what was going on.

Mary spoke to those who seemed to be the leaders and was told that they represented a peace group which rejected nuclear arms. It was the same objection that Mary had, with most of her pupils. The peace group told her that their society had failed to convince the officials and state leaders of the powers of destruction that the weapons represented.

In vain the group had submitted evidence with documents and photographs to show previous disasters involving nuclear weapons. Mary was given examples of the group's brochures and pamphlets, showing some of the evidence and the danger from nuclear armaments. She also saw that the group knew that the state had plans to use the weapons in the future.

One of the leaders noticed how much Mary and some of her pupils on the visit were taking an interest. He spoke to Mary and gave her a copy of videotape about their activities with the speeches of their leaders.

Mary realised that the protest was against a quantity of nuclear waste about to be removed from the plant, to be buried somewhere where it would constitute a danger to people. The group also objected to all forms of nuclear work, particularly the manufacture of weapons. Then May noticed that there was someone watching her and her pupils. She did not want any trouble with the police, she felt that they might be about to use force to control the crowds. So she decided to cancel the visit and return n to the school. She gathered those pupils who had left the bus and got them back on board. On the way back the students read the pamphlets they had been given, including one that said that the president of one country had threatened to destroy the world in five minutes-it was a joke.

Back at the school, Mary told the principal what had happened and said that it had been a lost opportunity to observe what really went on in the plant. She hoped that perhaps there would be another opportunity, and the principal said that she would try to organise another trip. This gave Mary the incentive to prepare for some action that would be heard all over the world. That demonstration had shown her she was not alone in her determination to stop it all. Many people-even those who had lost their husbands or had relatives serving abroad, people who were living lonely lives-these people were aware of the dangers that faced the world. At any time a war might break out and everything would be destroyed.

These people, Mary knew, were a support for her views. After seeing that demonstration she had concentrated all her thoughts on finding a way to free the world from the danger of nuclear war. Someone must set the alarm, someone who was prepared to make the sacrifice no matter what the effort required. The situation would not change by itself. In spite of all that the state provided for its people there was sadness and danger, the fear of the unknown. A large question mark sat before Mary.

The 8th Fleet arrived in the Mediterranean and approached the coast of Lebanon, opposite Beirut. It might move towards the Gulf of Arabia after the completion of the first mission. With David was another Marine who noticed that David was deeply troubled.

'What's the matter David?' Ed asked.

David sighed. 'Oh! Nothing really. I just can't help thinking about my pregnant wife back home!'

'Easy, David! Only a few more days and the mission will be completed and we'll be on the way home. You'll be back with your wife.'

David frowned. 'But we don't know what's going on, what will happen next?'

Ed tried to comfort him. 'Why be scared, you're a Marine! It's not the first time that we have achieved our target and got home safely!'

But David wasn't satisfied. 'Did you ask yourself about the mission? Why are we fighting someone else's battle? Here we are, thousands of miles from home. Who's going to benefit from it all? Why can't we live peacefully and leave the world in peace too?'

Then the alarm was sounded and they mustered to hear their next orders, to be told that they were to disembark the next day. The hours passed slowly. They could not rest and stood along the ship's rail staring at the land where they would be heading in the morning. It was, they thought, just a civil war in which they were involved. On land they could see the smoke of fire, the explosions of shells.

From the officers down, all ranks showed on their faces the strain of impending battle. They queued for dinner and when they had sat down, David said, 'Are we really going to protect the interest of our country here? And if so, what are those interests? Does the US or any American own any part of this place?'

A soldier called Bill looked at him. 'You just don't understand. We're here to prove to the world that we are her because we are powerful!'

'No, pal!' said another. 'You missed the whole point of the commanders. They won't tell us if we have friends here and that we have to defend them.'

Bill spoke again. 'There is another reason, it could be for some religious purpose. But it is not our target. Surely, religion means that all people are equal to God, so why should we kill anyone? We should be told who the offender is!'

Now, a sergeant jumped up and shouted, 'All this is none of your business. Let's eat! We take our orders and carry them out!' His tone upset many of the soldiers and one whispered, 'He doesn't want us to think for ourselves-and we come from the land of freedom, we salute the Statue of Liberty. Hail freedom!'

There was little sleep that night from anyone. One soldier sat all night smoking; another bit his nails; another stared at his family snapshots, tears running down his face. Near David was Ed, he said 'Are you still awake too?'

'Yes,' muttered Ed. 'I'm thinking of what's going to happen in the morning.'

'Same here! But someone should listen to what we have to say. We just have to talk to the commanders. They got voted in and control everything, our lives and all!'

Ed rolled over and stared at David. 'That's not your style and it's not the way a military man talks!'

David smiled. 'Don't get me wrong! I'm ready for what's coming but to tell you the truth I'm just not convinced by this mission in spite of all the information we get from the top. Inside, I feel there is something wrong. Wrong like some of the things that happened in other places where we have seen action. Are we repeating it all over?'

'I think we should stop talking and try to get some sleep,' suggested Ed.

Next morning they went on deck to see that the shore was much closer. They were ordered to climb down into the landing craft and were soon on their way towards the beach. There was no opposition and they marched inland towards the area they had been assigned to. The news of the landing was broadcast round the world, the state giving its justification for the action and saying that it was to establish peace and security in a land destroyed by civil war. They obviously hoped that the local inhabitants would believe all this and not put up any resistance. It did not work, for the people of that small country said they did not want any interference and were cautious about the occupying troops. The Marines were deployed into their positions and waited to see what would happen.

The news of the occupation was confusing and Mary was frightened and worried. She read and listened to the news and kept writing to David but never received anything back. It was a hard time for her. She did not get much sleep and took little food. The doctor told her that if she did not care of herself she might lose her baby.

The news grew worse. There was heavy fighting and the resistance was growing stronger. Then she got a letter from David, which eased her tension. The letter helped Mary a little, but the fact that David was fighting made her very worried. The inhabitants of the country David was in saw the soldiers as invaders. Mary thought that a mistake had been made, but she could not speak to anyone in authority about her fears.

She knew that she had to make some protest, do something that would be heard all over the world. To put an end to pain and grief. She would do it, but do what?

Mary lost her sense of time, of everything. One night the nation heard some important news. A huge convoy had penetrated the US base and detonated a large bomb. More than two hundred and fifty men were in the ruins, some perhaps still alive. Some of the injured had been dug out, seriously wounded. Mary, for once sleeping deeply, did not hear what had happened.

At school the next day, Mary was working calmly, the time passing slowly. She saw a military jeep drive into the school grounds and an officer and soldier get out. She saw their set faces and she knew that something had happened. They were hiding something, their eyes held nothing but pity. Her heart was pounding.

Then the Marine passed the door of the classroom where Mary was teaching and for a moment she thought that it was David. But the two men went straight to the head's office and a moment later she was called there too. She was afraid.

The officer hesitated. He wanted to say how sorry he was, but he managed to say that David had been dug from the wreckage of the building. He was injured and having treatment. Mary slipped to the floor in a faint. Her weakened condition did not help and she was rushed to hospital, where she remained for several days where they got some nourishment into her and gave her some pills to sleep.

She had visits from her school friends. They told her that the injured soldiers were soon to be brought to the hospital and Mary knew that she had to be strong.

To face whatever the futures had and above all to see David, no matter what his injuries were.

She was told that very soon she could go to David, when the aircraft arrived back in the country bringing him home. She knew that he had suffered serious injuries to the head, that some brain cells were damaged. The surgeons had operated to remove dead cells and she prepared herself to see David's deformed face.

On the day he was due back, Mary was ready to go to the airport. She was now quite big with her pregnancy, and still weak. While waiting she sat with one of the wife of the officers who had been killed-the mother of Richard. An army car came to pick them up and Richard and her older sister went with them, comforting their mother who cried all the way. Mary would see her husband, but the other woman's grief was far deeper.

She tried to say the right things to her. 'Did you accept it when your husband left?' she asked.

The crying woman said, 'I wasn't convinced deep down. I did not allow myself to think what my husband would be doing. Now all I have is grief and hatred for all what he has done.'

'Many men have sacrificed their lives for their homeland. We read so much about the homeland. For liberation, for unity, for defending us against invaders. We are not told, we never agreed to any intervention in a foreign land.'

Mary nodded. 'That's true. Intervention for humanitarian purposes or urgent assistance, there's no objection to that. But military intervention in the land's of others is not acceptable, even if it is made officially. Look what happened in Vietnam and is happening now in the Middle East.'

The driver had been listening to all this and he drew their attention to the fact that they were near the airport. He turned the radio on. It was describing the arrival of the dead and wounded, talking about the 'champions'. Mary asked the driver to tune into another station but the man hesitated.

'This is a free country!' Mary reminded him and the man turned to another radio station. It was giving interviews with members of the public on the tragedy that had happened, in preference to officials who wanted to put the government's views. It was obvious that demonstrations and protests were taking place all over the country.

High ranking officers were waiting to meet them at the gates and after expressing their sorrows to the relatives, they gave orders for soldiers to escort the relatives to seats in the hall. It was all done so smoothly that it seemed to Mary as if it had all been arranged long ago.

Then the aircraft was sighted and Mary prepared herself for the ordeal-an ordeal much worse for those knowing that all they would see would be coffins. The doors were opened and soldiers carried the coffins out one by one, marching slowly in time to a military band.

While the hearses drove away with the dead and their relatives, Mary was asked to wait for those injured who had been brought home. It seemed to take hours and Mary became scared and worried. Medical staff bustled about, followed by soldiers, some on two legs, others with crutches. Many were carried on stretchers, each one having his name read out and being met by his relatives.

Then Mary heard David's name. Fear took hold of her. She ran towards where he was to appear. Shocked, she saw someone who did not look like her husband, someone in a wheelchair, his head bowed, swathed in bandages. His right leg and foot were bandaged too. Then Mary saw the deformation to David's face.

Mary spoke to him. He tried to stand. Only his eyes moved, no other part of his body. Mary collapsed, this wasn't David. David had left in the form of a man, this was a human ruin.

When she recovered, she gathered her strength in order to take this human ruin back home with her. It was parts of a body-and two eyes, the only sign of what was once a man. He was little different from all those who had been brought back in coffins, except that his eyes were alive. Nothing else. Mary felt almost tempted to run away, to go mad. But she had to be faithful, this was all she had.

Officers came over to talk to her. They said that he would be awarded medals and that his treatment would continue. She heard but did not take it all in, only that she would meet them again.

A special escort helped them to a car. David was helped out of his wheelchair and into the car. All the way home, Mary looked at David as if he were a broken doll, a machine. She put memories of the past, of what David once was, behind her. What he was now was a deformed, disabled thing. That was his future as well as hers.

What lay ahead? A hard time, continuous pain. How could she manage with a disabled husband? Could she leave him every day to go to her school? She cried and the escort was so sorry for them. He offered to take David not to his home but to a clinic where Mary could visit him from time to time.

Mary's eyes blazed. 'No! No! No! You took his body. Now leave me his soul!'

Sadly, the escort knew he had said the wrong thing and turned away.

All the time, Mary had been holding David's hands. Suddenly his face turned to hers and tears ran down from the wide-open red-rimmed eyes. She sensed his anger and she put her arms round him and their tears ran together between their faces.

Mary clung to David until they reached home. She helped him in and the door shut behind them. It was like a curtain closing or a book shutting, the final chapter of a family's life. Life would now be behind that shut door. Slowly, Mary recovered, their heir would not be a grave, she had to maintain David's condition as best as she could. He was now the reason for rescuing the world and its people from certain danger, to start with him a new chapter.

What could she do?

The days fell past, as regular as the leaves from the trees in autumn. Mary never lost hope, she had the feeling that something would happen, that one day the world would be different. She knew too that the birth of her baby was getting near and took care of herself. It might be the event upon which her aspirations would flourish.

Would her child be an intellectual, a great scientist who would end war and the pain of humanity, spreading peace round the world? But life was hard and time was short. The state might go to war and would she live through it? There was little pleasure in the contemplation of the future.

More and more, Mary put despair behind her and concentrated on David. It was he who needed her now. Every time she looked at his poor face she thought of those peace movements in and outside her country. She contacted people and gained more supporters. The protests continued but they were not enough for Mary. She wanted something special-for ordinary peace meetings failed. Then she remembered something else, something that she had previously felt guilty about-revenge. The idea drove her on, even when she looked at the sleeping form of her husband; even when she was at school. Revenge had taken control.

But Mary became worried about her feelings, so much so that she visited a psychiatrist. Her feelings about revenge were against her morals and her religion. Unfortunately the psychiatrist was of no help and she felt more and more disturbed. She needed to rid herself of her anger or she would hurt someone or damage something. It had to be some action that would draw the people's attention to the dangers and save the lives of millions.

One day, returning from yet another visit to the psychiatrist, she heard that the President was going to visit the town and talk to the people. He was trying to gain support for his second term, and his speech would be part of the campaign.

On the day, Mary stood in the crows and saw the President stand to begin his speech. He spoke of the glory of the country, and with every word Mary's resentment grew stronger. David's story said something different, the opposite of those carefully selected presidential words. Mary felt as if she ought to turn into a bomb and leap up on to the stand and bring an end to the speech.

Mary's emotions became so strong that she fainted, crumpling in a heap and surrounded by people. There were shouts for help and police were called who picked her up and carried her to the cover of the dais where the president was. The policemen who were supposed to be looking after Mary started listening to the president and just stood there. As Mary slowly recovered she saw the policemen standing by her. Then she saw his gun.

Here was her long-awaited chance, the way for her to express her resentment and fury and the tragedy of her life.

The crowd heard the shots that rang out and uproar broke out. The president stopped talking as his bodyguards quickly surrounded him. She still held the policeman's gun and then she shot the president. Police and bodyguards ran to arrest her. She wanted to tell the people that she had done it to bring justice. The president's words were false and if he wanted to see the truth he should come to her house and see it. Unable to control herself, Mary fainted again. People stood round her, seeing the gun in her hand.

Then the crowd laughed, hearing the fireworks. Mary woke from her dream.

Still lying down, but conscious, Mary talked to those round her, she told them of her dream, wanting everyone to know how she wanted to make her point to the world, as if to say, 'If you are not aware now, your turn will come to be a victim'.

She felt as if she had taken the place of the president on the stand and spoke of the prevailing policies that would not lead the world to peace.

'The super-powers have the responsibility of establishing peace, they are the only ones who can ease or mould events in the world. But the super-powers are behind many of the troubles, coups and civil wars. They interfere with the powers of others, using their money. They could help lesser people develop without dominating their lives and controlling their destiny.'

Mary was still talking. 'Consider what you are doing, time is against you. You should make friends rather than enemies round the world. Preserve your country before interfering in the lands of others. Put an end to nuclear weapons with their power of world destruction. They can start a third world war and destroy the world all in the name of power. Let super-powers remain but let them pay for their errors. The whole world will regret that nuclear powers were ever manufactured.

'Shall we wake up and put things right before it's too late? That's all I have to say. Thank you for listening!'

Mary heard the crowd beginning to clap and they continued to clap and cheer without stopping. Mary was congratulated on her speech as she waved to the crowd and walked through the people. She was lifted onto the shoulders of a man and woman and with the crowd following was carried to a car waiting to take her home.

It was more astonishing that Mary found herself not surprised to see David actively joining in the campaign against the dangers and effects of nuclear war. He admired what she had been saying, and asked to hear more. Then he helped her into the car and drove away.

Mary noticed strange and extraordinary things happening round her. The car was somehow expanding, its seats were changing into beds. There were sounds like those a siren makes. And then the most bizarre thing of all…David's features were changing. He was a stranger.

'Who are you?' asked Mary.

The man looked at her and answered, 'I am the first-aid man.'

Mary looked the other way and saw beside her the policeman who had been escorting her when she was near the podium on which the President had stood.

In a daze, Mary realised that it was all some kind of trance, a dream. She had heard that clapping, but it was the applause of the people for the president, not for her words to them.

But the policemen seemed so real. She spoke to him. 'Where am I? Where are we going?'

The man said, 'This is an ambulance and you are on your way to the hospital. In your condition you should not have been there to listen to the President's speech!' In a strange half-time between the real and the imagined, Mary had accomplished something, which she could not have done, in reality.

She had failed. No one had heard her, no one had applauded. She had not been carried from the meeting on the shoulders of people who were cheering and clapping for her. Here she was in an ambulance and disappointment kept her quiet, surrendering herself to her fate. This is how she would have to live-the reality away from her dreams and hopes.

At the hospital Mary was quickly examined and the doctor advised her not to become involved in any crisis, telling her she should not strain herself for the sake of the baby due to be born so soon.

Rejecting offers and suggestions that she should stay overnight in hospital, Mary asked someone to take her home and she was grateful to them. It had been a long, hard day. She was late and she did not want to be accused of neglecting her duty to her husband. Such actions might be used as an excuse to take her husband away.

She embraced David, sorry that she had not fed him properly that day. Food was soon prepared and David was made to understand why she had been away for so long. He wanted Mary to know that he thought she was looking well and had a lot of questions to ask. It took him a long while to voice them while she reassured him, saying that she was late because of being delayed at the hospital. Tired, she went to bed, she must have some sleep before morning.

The next day, as usual, Mary made David comfortable and left things at hand for him in her absence. There was a bell on his wheelchair which could summon help from next door if any emergency arose. On the way out she as always called on her neighbour and asked her to keep an ear out for David's alarm. It was one piece of modern technology which Mary took advantage of, although in general she was against all such things.

Not surprisingly, Mary's life had been so disrupted that it was affecting her work. Her students noticed that the lessons she took were becoming boring but sympathized trying to understand the problems of pregnancy, the extra work she had to do at home coping with David's helplessness.

Mary noticed that one student had been absent for the second of two periods, even though she was somewhere in the school. It was Sarah. Two other students were absent too, one being Simon, the other Richard. Simon had been excused but not Richard, who it seemed, had no excuse.

Mary wondered where Sarah was. One student thought she might be in the garden, but Mary had to know. She had received a letter from a student who lived next door to Richard who was also absent and it was worrying.

When the class was over, Mary hurried out to the garden, hoping to find Sarah there. At first she could not see any sign of the girl, but then she heard the sound of crying coming from behind a tree. As Mary approached, the weeping girl thrust a piece of paper behind her.

'Let me see that!' ordered Mary and reluctantly the girl handed it to her. 'I don't want Richard to die, can we save him?' sobbed Sarah.

When Mary had finished readi1ng the letter she asked where Richard was and was he serious? Sarah said yes he was, he was grieved over the death of his father who had been killed in action in Lebanon.

Mary took Sarah back to the school and told her wait while she collected her car. On the way she met Catherine who wanted to know where she was going in such a hurry.

'Is it to do with David?' she asked.

Saying that she hoped so, Mary drove away leaving Catherine to wonder what she meant.

On their way, Mary asked Sarah about Richard's suicidal action. 'Doesn't he realise how many casualties it will lead to?' she said.

'He's been thinking of doing something drastic ever since he heard of his father's death. But why should he kill himself? And others because he says they were the cause of his father's death?'

'He wants to stop it like I want to stop it,' said Mary. 'On the day the body of Richard's fathers came back draped in the flag, they returned my own husband. He is crippled and almost dead. But revenge is wrong as well as suicide. Damage is not made right by more damage. Killing is not stopped by more killing. It is all unfair!'

She drove fast towards the nuclear base. It was often attacked by people who crowded round it protesting against what was being produced there. this time was different. There was a deadly danger, for the student was on his way to detonate a shipment of nuclear missiles that were about to be sent to a port and from there to a country in Europe.

The details of his actions had been sent in a letter to Sarah, his girlfriend and classmate. They had to find Richard. Still driving fast, Mary asked herself how Richard could even think of doing this idiotic thing? How had he obtained the necessary fuel and the gas pipes that he had installed in his father's car?

Sarah said that Richard had planned it some time ago, soon after his father's funeral.

I didn't think he was serious! I thought he was just angry. But when I got this letter I realised that he wasn't joking.'

'How did he prepare for it?'

'He just spent hours and hours in his father's garage. And used all his money on buying pipes and chemicals.'

'In his letter what did he mean about the gas pipes that had been installed everywhere in the car?'

'He fixed pipes in the front of the car so they will detonate when the car collides with the truck loaded with the weapons.'

'How did Richard know about the timing of the movements of this truck carrying the shipment?'

'There were important documents that Richard's father had hidden in his files. Including details about the transport of nuclear missiles that are scheduled to take place in the future. Richard wants to follow his father who died while attacking the HQ in Lebanon.'

But Richard did not know the difference between the two situations and the fatal error he was committing.

The nuclear plant was close now and Mary slowed down. She asked Sarah where they might find Richard and the girl said they could try a nearby side-road where she could see a car that looked like the one that had belonged to Richard's father. But it was not the correct car. So Mary continued to drive round the walls of the plant, trying to find the car Richard had been driving.

Then they saw the carrier of the missiles parked beside the gate, with an HQ car and two others parked behind it. Mary suddenly realised that she had been looking in the wrong place near the main gate. But before she could start the engine they found themselves surrounded by several other vehicles. She knew that it was time for the missile shipment to move off-and Richard was still hiding somewhere. There must be a way of preventing what Richard was trying to do, and she wanted to stop him without letting the authorities know.

At the very least this would lead to the boy being sent to prison. Mary did not want to destroy the boy's future by exposing his secret. This meant that she couldn't tell the guards the real reason why she was driving round the plant.

The first thing the guards asked her was, 'What are you doing here at this time?'

The best thing Mary could do was act naturally and appear totally relaxed. 'I am a teacher at the secondary school and this girl is one of my students. We came here to look for an appropriate campsite for our school trip that is due soon.'

Thankfully, Mary saw that the guards became more relaxed, so she added that the students would be spending two days there, adding an apology for bothering them.

The man in charge became courteous then and said that it was all just a routine check Mary asked then if they had seen a large white car anywhere near, which seemed to have lost its way. He had seen the car passing the fence round the base, he said. Then it disappeared among the trees opposite the main gate. Mary asked him why there was more than one gate for such an important and dangerous area.

'That's easy to answer. The second gate is used for trucks and working parties and not visitors. When you come to see us, please come to the main gate.'

Now Mary knew where the reckless young Richard was lurking, waiting for the shipment. She also saw the engines of the trucks being run up.

She felt very tense, but tried to hide it from the guards even though they might find the truth out very soon. She managed to keep cool and calm until the guards moved away. It was, of course, important not to leave before them. That might arouse suspicion. The matter was nearly beyond her control and she nearly revealed it all when the trucks began to move towards the gate, before stopping for final safety checks. They appeared to be waiting for an officer who was to be in charge of the convoy.

These were the last moments if the situation was to be saved and Richard kept out of extreme trouble. Mary drove towards the gate slowly, seeing the officer getting into his car and giving the other drivers to move off. And then the convoy was in motion. Now Mary had to accelerate for the car driven by Richard might appear at any moment along the side-road hidden by the trees.

Sarah screamed. 'There he is!'

They saw the white car on the move and Mary put her foot down and raced past the convoy. She nearly crashed into one vehicle and they heard the driver curse. But Mary drove on intending to overtake the leading car, which tried to stop her. He switched his siren on to make her stop but she ignored it.

Richard's car was approaching and Mary slid to a stop by the main entrance. They got out and she and Sarah stood in the middle of the road to block the way of the white car rushing towards the convoy.

Would he run them over? They were his two most loved people!

They saw his stricken face as he stared at his girlfriend and his teacher. What should he do? Should he kill Mary and Sarah before crashing into the convoy? He now had two choices in his terrible one-track mission. He chose the last.

The matter was over.

4

They left the danger zone in dead silence. Sarah stared angrily at Richard but her expression soon eased and softened and finally she spoke to him.

'Why did you do it? Did you really want to leave me alone? Didn't you think past it, what might have happened if you had caused that terrible explosion? You would have a really hard time if they had caught you, you'd never be left alone!'

But Richard shook his head, he was adamant. 'I should have killed them; never let them make any more of the things!'

Then Mary said, 'That would make you just a criminal, to be locked away for many years and lost to the cause of peace. Look, Richard, think it over, be careful!'

'Think about it! They can kill us without worrying about it. So should we stop and think before we kill them?'

Mary said that of course they ought to be condemned as terrorists and criminals working against peace. Why should we give them the opportunity to call us criminals? That would not be the image we want to raise. It all calls for careful planning and thinking.

'What we have to do,' is use their plans against them. To show the world that we stand for peace, that we aren't criminals only intent on killing and destruction. We don't want to oppress anyone.

Every time Mary stopped talking there was dead silence. She heard Richard sigh and Sarah looked thoughtful, probably feeling isolated.

'Well?' said Mary, looking at her students in turn.

Sarah shook her head. 'I just can't understand how Richard could do this!'

'But surely you can't think that Richard and I are wrong in our condemnation of our dictators, our efforts to establish peace?'

'Of course I understand! But can we face them all?'

Richard now broke the silence he had held. 'You see, Sarah, we must face them, the leaders, but how do we do it. We have no power, no equality with them.'

Mary thought that she should produce some kind of answer. 'We may not be as powerful as them. But our will is stronger and our numbers are huge. All people want peace, no one wants to be humiliated, destroyed!'

Sarah took heart at what Mary was saying. 'So we must somehow confront them, bring them to trial and charge them with crimes against humanity. Courts are the place where justice is delivered and we have clear evidence to prove what we say!'

Richard shook his head, he didn't think that the law was powerful enough to condemn the state for what it was doing. The state controlled the law as it did everything.

'Whatever the cost,' Mary insisted, 'we have to bring them up for trial in the courts, to expose them. The idea of a trial is wonderful! We can accuse them without being branded criminals. We have the right to do it and if they don't give us that right they will soon know what else we can do!'

They were now back and Richard went to his home to find his mother crying. 'Why!' she sobbed, 'Why? Were you going to leave me as your poor father did? When your sister told me what you were going to do I nearly telephoned the police so that they would stop you. But I didn't because I thought that they would hurt you!'

Richard said how sorry he was that he had left his mother this way and tried to comfort her. And Mary told her that Richard would never do such a thing again, she would make sure of that. 'He's just got to think before he does anything like that before!' she finished.

The boy's mother put her arms round him. Mary knew how much comfort she needed after the loss of her husband-and Richard need to forget what he had done and be the man of the house.

Mary left them. It had been a worrying and frightening time, but it was life. Men and women were complicated creatures with mixed emotions and hearts which never lost the wish for pleasure and sympathy. The world's leaders wanted to suppress these natural feelings. She hoped that good would eventually win over evil, and justice would defeat wrongs. Peace just has to win, thought Mary.

Mary and Sarah drove away in silence, each deep in their own thoughts, until they not speak reached Sarah's house, where she got out smiling and confident. She did not but they smiled at each other as Mary drove off. Mary drove to the garage to have her car put right, still unhappy, and still angry. At home David in his wheelchair as usual, doing nothing. Thinking-what?

She kissed him and ran her hands through his hair comforting, loving. He tried to touch the long blonde hair cascading down her back, but his paralysed hand would not move. Mary knew what he was trying to do and it hurt. Then he managed to move his head enough to kiss the top of her head, her hair. She knew that he was trying to show his sorrow, that it was all he could do.

Mary could not stop the tears, but she kissed his hands, she smiled sadly. This was all that was left of their feelings towards each other, the difference between now and the husband he was before he left. She said 'Have you eaten, David and taken your medicine?'

He managed to nod again Mary smiled in response to this, heartened that they could at least communicate 'Keep on taking your medicine' she said, pretending to be stern. 'One day you will be well again and return to life, be your old self. And get to know our child which is coming soon!'

Another nod from David, but what was he really trying to say. One nod is like another, there is no meaning. He was a hopeless case, she knew that. He would never recover from the paralysis, which gripped him. All she could do was help to relive his physical and mental suffering.

Mary stood up. 'I must go and my clothes and get lunch ready.' She laughed, but David's head had dropped to its usual position. Before lunch and after finishing the jobs about the house, Mary went next door for a few minutes to ask what David had eaten and if he had rejected his medicine as usual Her neighbour said that he never howed any interest in food or his medicine.

She went back indoors in case David needed her. He had no one else, no one to care for him except her. She was his only support. She moved him in his wheelchair in front of the window so that he could see the garden, the place where they used to have so much fun. Then she concentrated on preparing the lesson for the next day's lectures at school.

The next morning, Mary got breakfast for the two of them and called on Margaret to ask her to look after David while she was at school. This she was happy to do every day when she took her baby for a walk.

Mary called at the garage and collected her car, which had had the dents in it hammered out, drove to school where she found Richard waiting at the door. He had not gone in to join his friends and seemed confused, but at least he managed to say good morning to Mary as she approached.

'What are you standing there for, Richard'

'I just couldn't sleep last night. I kept thinking of putting the word's leaders on trial, stopping them. But I think there are other ways too! Why don't we send letters to the newspapers and try to support for our ideas?'

Mary shook her head. 'What you fail to realise is that the newspapers are owned by powerful people. They wouldn't print our letters and if they did we would find ourselves in trouble. No, trail is the best way, the only way where we have right.'

But this did not convince Richard, who said that he was really in a hurry, he wanted revenge.

'Richard, take it easy!' ordered Mary, 'We'll sort it all out in time. Now let's get into the classroom.'

She went in, with Richard following, and said hello to her pupils. She had prepared a quiz for the middle of the period to see how they were doing and get some feedback from them.

Mary had just begun her lecture when the door opened and the school principal came in. 'How are things going?' she asked Mary, who said that everything was OK and the principal looked at the pupils to see that their reaction was. Mary saw that they all looked relaxed a happy and the principal said that at the end of the week they would be going on a three-day trip.

'The first day will be a visit to the nuclear power station and you will be camping in the forest close by. Your teacher will be supervising you of course.'

When the principal had gone, Mary asked her pupils for their opinion on the trip. It was clear that they were pleased and felt it had come at the right time. There seemed to be some element of secrecy in their faces now that they knew they would be going to the plant again.

Mary left the classroom at the end of the session and Mark who was now obsessed with the idea of eliminating oppression and that he wanted to do more than just see this nuclear weapons went up to Richard in his quiet way. He whispered that he wanted to do more than just see this nuclear plant. He wanted to get hold of the weapons and damage them, put them out of action for good.

'So do I!' Richard agreed.

Then Edward joined them and asked Richard where he had been the day before, was he ill?

'I want out to the plant on a suicide mission, Edward!' 'It went wrong but if I had succeeded it would have solved all our problems!'

'Suicide? What on earth are you talking about?

Richard explained how he had taken his father's car and set an ambush for a truck loaded with nuclear weapons. He wanted to explode it, to destroy it, but Mary and Sarah had interrupted him second before he carried his plan out. He asked Edward if he agreed with him about what he wanted to do.

Then Mark asked why Richard had not told them. They were friends and it was a wonderful idea even though it had gone wrong.

'We all support you, Richard! WE would have all joined you. We should all work together to bring these manufacturers of nuclear weapons to court.'

But Mark wanted to know who would hold the trial and where it would take place.

'Who will support us?'

Mary told herself that what she had to have was patience. She spent the rest of the day taking care of David and preparing the lecture notes for the next day's lessons.

The quietness of night covered a sad house. No voices at bedtime, for going to bed was done in silence. Perhaps he did but his paralysed tongue would not allow him to. So she lay there thinking of the trial of the world, for peace everywhere and she slept.

As usual, Mary woke and rose to prepare breakfast for them both. She gave David his medicine. She spoke to him.

'I'm going to teach the wicked people in this world a lesson! They have changed my life, all I have is silence. I'm going to expose their rimes-and you are my proof?'

David heard her. His eyes were worried, she knew. He could not answer, but his eyes seemed to say, 'Wait! I don't want revenge, enough is enough. They won't show you mercy!' His eyes were now apologetic, pleading. Mary knew what he was trying to say, but she just could not agree.

All she could do was say, 'But I'm not going to fight them with weapons, I'm not going to kill anyone. Their punishment will come from the law at the end of the trail. The voice of right will be louder than that of evil.'

She saw David's eyes. He wanted to stop her, to tell her that it was impossible, that powerful men would stop her.

For a few moments Mary said nothing, tears trickled down her cheeks. Then she said, 'I don't fear their power, nor will I run. They must listen sooner or later. They have deprived us and many others of our happiness, our security, so why should I leave them in peace? They must be suppressed, uprooted, eradicated. Justice must win!'

Mary, still talking to herself, stood up and pushed David's wheelchair into the living room. Justice must be done…oppression must be eradicated…people must sleep well and peacefully…we must punish them, make them realise that we reject nuclear armament and demand peace…

She called on Margaret as usual, asking her to drop in from time to time just to make sure David was all right. Then she walked to her car. The matter of the trial was becoming an obsession with her, it thinking of all the probabilities. The trial would be the real solution. She would support her students in condemning power and save the poor from oppression. She drove in a preoccupied way and nearly dented it on a lorry stopped at some lights.

She went to the teacher's room for a cup of coffee then, without a word in answer to Catherine's greeting, went straight to her classroom. Her lesson was organized so that she could question her pupils afterwards. After the session she reminded them of the departure time of the visit to the nuclear power station.

'Don't be late and be ready to spend a week in camp. Take one of these instruction leaflets before you go.'

Before she could get away Sarah and Richard stopped her. They wanted to see her in the afternoon to ask her about the base, what questions they could raise, and that they hoped that it would be possible to hold the trial.

'Yes, you can come see me this afternoon,' Mary said. 'It'll have to be at home, before we leave on our trip. So I'll see you later!'

On their way home, Sarah and Richard met Edward and Mark. They walked together and told them that they were going to meet Mary later at her house.

'What do you think of the weekend visit?' Mark asked Sarah.

'It'll be exciting-a change from hard work at school.'

But Richard wanted to discuss more important matters, about nuclear disarmament.

Mark said he had a few good questions too.

'But I wanted to ask Mary about them first. Can Edward and I go with you and Sarah to see Mary too?'

They decided that it would be alright since they were all very much concerned about peace and nuclear weapons.

Mary had a busy time preparing sufficient meals for David, putting them in the freezer so that Margaret could keep David fed properly. Then she sat down and lunched with David, telling him that some of her students were coming to see her to talk to her about the visit to the plant and camping nearby. She said that he could stay and listen to their discussion.

Mary wanted David to see that the next generation rejected nuclear arms and wars. There was nothing he could do of course, not even get out of his wheelchair. Lunch finished, she relaxed for a while until the phone rang. It was Edward asking if he and Mark could come with Sarah and Richard.

'Of course,' she said.

She put the phone down and went out into the garden that had not been tended for so long. She stayed there until she saw the four students coming down the road. She led them into the living room where they were shocked and surprised to see poor David there-crippled and so badly paralyzed, a body unable to move.

They looked uncomfortable, but Mary put them at ease.

'This is my husband David.'

To her surprise she heard a sound come from him that was just understandable. A hesitant, 'Hello!'

It was the first thing he had said since coming home! And then she saw one hand move, he was trying to greet them! He was defying his disability and Mary knew that loving him and caring had not been enough. He had to be driven to make efforts to speak and move.

The four students and Mary sat down round the table, with David in his wheelchair close by. Still shattered and delighted by David's first word and realised the idea of peace had force the sound out of his mouth, Mary knew that he would be with them. Once desperate he was now hopeful and it made Mary even more determined than before. David was the torch, which would show her the way out of the darkness of the nuclear age.

For a moment the students were silent, aware that David's voice had been something dramatic, a sign of his support for them. They saw that Mary was in ecstasy about her husband's sudden show of life. But she forced herself to attend to her students' questions. They wanted to know if they could stay there or go to the school and would they disturb David if they stayed?

Before she could speak she saw David nod his head.

'Don't worry', she told them, 'He's more interested than any of us!'

5

Danger and the unknown now faced the three boys and the girl hidden, observing. They watched movements on the site, the control room, the HQ and the power plant. It was comparatively easy to hide, but much more difficult to observe men moving about, to know about the operating system on the base and take it over. Two boys with radios were in the ventilation ducts. One, the leader, passed instructions to the other, who made his way carefully to the lad in the book and data cupboard, hiding on the upper shelves among files and papers. His small form helped him-anyone large would not have been able to conceal himself there.

The plot was nearly exposed when an officer came in to take one of the files. The hidden boy moved slightly and dislodged some papers, which slithered on the floor. Another man looked in to see what was wrong but he did not stay. The presence of someone in that small cupboard was the last thing they anticipated! The officer picked the papers up an, because he would have to find a ladder to reach the top shelf, he placed them on a lower one to save himself the trouble.

As work went on at the base, Mary kept in touch with the four by means of the walkie-talkie. She did it from near the area where the boys' tents were sited on one side of the lake, with the girls on the other side. Within two hours from leaving the base, Mary was speaking to the boys, hearing what was happening and giving her orders to them.

Mary warned them to avoid becoming impatient but to wait until the men working in the base became bored and tired with what was sometimes monotonous work. The lads kept watch, seeing how the men operated the equipment and carried out tasks in the control room.

But just when all seemed to be going to plan, Mary heard the sirens on the base begin to sound, alerting the soldiers, who ran to their stations. Richard called Mary on his walkie-talkie and said he could not see what the trouble was but they had not been discovered.

The sirens stopped for a few minutes, then started again. The four pupils prepared themselves for a run to safety; they felt rightly that they were great danger. Then they saw that the base commander had obviously given an order to check the HQ and start the process of missile readiness. He went into the control room and immediately showed signs of suspicion.

His jaws moving on chewing gum, the commander walked towards the large bin where Mark was hiding and lifted the lid. The boy held his breath, ready for the shout and the guns. But the commanders did nothing but spit the wad of gum out and bark an order.

'OK! Its all clear, so stop the sirens and give the all clear!'

The rest of the soldiers relaxed and began to switch on the communication and observation systems, the cameras and audio systems.

As the sirens died down, everyone felt easier. The boys realised that it had been a routine test just to make sure everyone on the base was alert, able to repel any terrorist attack. They heard the commander make his announcement through the loud speakers, giving his thanks for the good performance of everyone on the base.

Sarah and Richard, hiding in their ventilation duct, knew that the workers were doing routine tasks. In contact with Mary, Richard asked if they could start their operation as everything seemed to be calm.

There was no reply immediately from Mary, but then one of the operators suddenly shouted that a copy of the launching and control plan was missing. Everyone started looking round to try to find the document, not imagining that it could have been stolen. If someone could get in to take it, it raised real problems for security. And whoever had it would be able to threaten the whole world.

When the document was not found, the security people were called, who alerted the base commander. He gave orders that everyone who had been on the previous shift should be traced and questioned. Again, the four hidden students felt that they were about to be found and arrested.

Richard tried to contact Mary but failed once more. Sarah gave him the plans and asked him toward the control room and take it over, then start the missile launching procedure.

'Hurry!' she said, 'I'll keep trying to contact Mary!' The lad nodded and gave a whispered goodbye, then moved off down the ventilation duct to join the other two.

A team of security men had been moving about but they failed to find anything suspicious, so they gave the OK and said the plans could not be anywhere in the building. Their leaders said that it was probable that the plans had somehow been leaked out of the base and that a special meeting was to be called to discuss the situation. One of the soldiers said that a class of students had visited the base earlier and had insisted on entering the control room. One girl had shown a lot of interest and it might have been she who had taken the copy of the plans.

While the meeting was important, the base commander did not want to report it to his higher commander before finding and questioning the class who had visited the control room that morning.

Search parties went out and calls were made on the school, but it was a holiday and there were no teachers there. Then they got the address of the supervisor and went to her house but she was off for the weekend with her husband. Then the soldiers tried to find out the names of the visiting class and their teacher and had to break into the school at night to get the names.

A section of soldiers were sent to ask the parents of the students where they were and this frightened the fathers and mothers. They were told that one of the students was lost, but the parents had heard nothing about it and said that they were sure that all the students and the teacher were camping near the lake.

It was now nighttime but this information sent the searching team straight to the lakeside with a description of the girl who had shown so much interest in the launching plans. The vehicles were parked by the lake and the soldiers moved through the darkened trees in search of the students' camp. It was eerie in the dark forest and the soldiers were on edge. Suddenly they were attacked, one soldier firing his gun at the shadowy figures with no effect. But it was only young boys playing games and the soldier apologized for using his weapon.

On the other side of the lake, Mary heard the sound of the gun firing. She thought that the plot had been discovered but then she decided not to call it off. It was as if some invisible power was supporting her, telling her that she was in the right and that she had to go on. In her mind was the picture of David, the victim. She radioed the boys telling them to put the plan into operation, but first to hide the walkie-talkie.

A few minutes later the search party came into the campsite, asking for the person who was in charge. Mary came forward and he said he wanted to search the camp and question all the girls. She objected to this, saying that the girls were all sleeping. Her objection was ignored and the officer in charge told his soldiers to search the tents where the girls were in their sleeping bags.

Mary was very angry, she said the girls were young and not properly dressed, it was an outrage. She was then allowed to wake the girls and wait while they got dressed. She was told to line them up to be questioned. Each group stood in front of its tent and the officer began by checking the girls' faces against the description he had been given. Mary knew, of course, but said nothing.

When three of the four tents had been searched, the soldiers were approaching the fourth when Mary was astonished to see Sarah! She saw that the girl was breathing heavily and her shoes and clothes were very dirty, but the officer did not seem to notice the difference between Sarah and the rest of the girls. He wanted to see her bags and she pointed into the tent.

When he came out he had found nothing and apologized to Mary who still showed her anger at the intrusion. The officer and his soldiers left the camp area and when they were back in their vehicles their HQ was contacted and told that nothing of importance had been found.

When all was quiet again, Mary hugged Sarah. Had the officer found that the number of girls was one less he would have been alerted that something was wrong. She took Mary inside her tent and said that the boys had been told to carry out their mission and that she would join them when they had taken over the base.

Mary was so surprised to see Sarah that she had not immediately asked her how she had tome back to the camp, where her presence certainly eased the situation. But as soon as she could she began questioning her closely.

In the dark, Sarah had got through the ventilation ducts into the outer hall, then she saw that a truck was about to leave and she climbed into the back and hid behind some boxes.

Twice, Sarah was nearly discovered. Once when the guards stopped the truck at the gates but did not take the trouble to make a proper search. And the second time when Mary made a sound as she tried to jump off, but the truck accelerated and the girl had to dive back behind the boxes. The driver got out to see what the sound was but again did not look behind the boxes. When the truck did at last stop and the soldiers got out to urinate, Sarah crept out and ran into the bushes.

In the dark, Sarah ran through the bushes and trees being scratched and knocked by branches as she headed away from the base and toward the lake where she knew the campsite lay. Just as she neared the camp she saw that there were soldiers searching it, but she took her place in line with her friends.

So Mary and Sarah sat, praying that the boys would succeed in their so dangerous mission.

Back in the base, Richard checked his position and saw that it was all right to emerge from his hiding place. There was a feeling between the boys that they knew what their friends were doing even when they were apart. As if there were a supporting presence acknowledging that theirs was a good and just cause. They had tried to understand it before but there seemed to be no logical explanation. It was a form of truth, an absolute sense of responsibility.

David was always in their minds. He was standing by them, another member of their team, working with them and sharing their ideals. But they saw him as he had once been-well and fit, a soldier in battle. Not the poor, crippled victim ruined by war.

In the control room everything was normal when Richard gave the signal for action. The three boys left their hiding places and quietly approached the control staff, their faces protected by masks. Then they leapt forward and sprayed the men with the gas and the men immediately collapsed on to the floor. One of the boys had to struggle with an officer and when his face-protection slipped he was slightly affected by the spray. The officer still struggled and hit to be hit hard on the head with a telephone, knocking him unconscious.

The men were dragged to one side, tied up and their mouths sealed with adhesive tape, then the outer door was locked and the inner control room secured by having its programmed locks operated. The next job was too de-activating the TV security cameras and other surveillance equipment.

It was as if the boys had been working as a closely-knit team for years. They had strength and conviction, which enabled them to complete the main part of the launch operation with the mainframe computer supplying all the answers to any problems that arose.

Now all was ready and there was a moment of silence as the boys looked at each other, then at Richard, waiting for him to declare a war of peace and to announce a new power in the world.

Richard knew that his moment had come. He thought of Mary, his friends, David, his father, all those who had been killed by nuclear weapons. He also thought of the victims of every war and every country. The boys reached out to touch hands, swearing to press on without hesitation.

Then Richard stepped forward and entered the order on the computer to move the missiles. Seconds later there were movements outside the control room and the siren began to sound. A telephone rang and a voice from the loudspeaker asked what was going on in there. The voice warned that it was dangerous and illegal to run the apparatus this way. Then the voice ordered the doors to be open but it was naturally ignored.

'Launching nuclear missiles without order from the high commander is prohibited!' came out of the loudspeakers.

For the second time, the officer in charge of the shift contacted his superiors. For him the situation was now out of control and he was afraid. Outside the control room men were beginning to worry that there had been an attack from an enemy who had entered the base. Beyond the walls of the base, high-ranking officers were on their way to take control.

When they arrived they wanted to start negotiations with whoever was inside the control room. Round the loudspeakers the boys handed Richard the microphone, but he gave it to Edward.

'Disguise your voice and tell them that all the high commands in the country must come to talk.

Edward's assumed voice cracked through the loudspeaker that negotiations would take place in the meeting hall. The boys, from the safety of the control room would talk through microphones, and TV cameras would show them and their state of readiness to proceed at all stages.

There seemed to be no alternative, so the high-ranking officers were summoned to the base. The boys were asked to reveal their identities and list all their demands. Or stop what they were doing and come out. They were warned that their actions were dangerous.

Edward used his disguised voice again, saying that they would wait until everyone was present. As the time passed the boys completed their work on the computer and other systems and switches.

Richard thought of contacting Mary but decided that it was too dangerous. She might be caught with the walkie-talkie and bugging systems had probably been brought in to detect any kind of communication between the inside and others outside the base. The men tied up had recovered consciousness and were struggling. The boys removed their handguns and then gave each man an injection to put him back to sleep for about twenty-four hours.

Over the microphone, the boys said that they would reveal their identities as soon as they were sure that all the high commands and people from the Ministry of Defense were present and that the head of the country had been fully informed of what was happening. They knew, too, that there were many journalists outside the plant who were trying to find out what was going on there?

It was announced that the talks would begin within an hour. But Richard needed to preserve their position and so he arranged to have some short-range missiles made ready. This brought a response from outside, saying that the command was ready, so would they stop moving any more missiles into readiness.

It seemed that the whole world had very quickly learned about the events at the nuclear base, about the unidentified people who had taken control of the missiles. In the camp outside, Mary and Sarah could not sleep. Then they heard the wailing of the sirens again and they knew that the boys had taken the control room.

Mary prayed that the boys would achieve their ambitions but had to act as if things were normal in the camp. She woke the girls for their morning exercise as if this were the most important event of the day. But she kept an ordinary radio turned on, for special programs were being broadcast covering the incident.

She still wanted to go to David and tell him what was happening, and she wanted to go to the boys. But she decided to stay in the camp and pretend all was well, even though her mind was in a continual turmoil. By now, the boys would have prepared the statement that they would declare their identities and spell out their demands, the statement that she had outlined. Whatever the cost to them, they would carry it out.

In her tent, Sarah was sitting alone, thinking and worrying about her friends and their possible fate and regretting that she had left them, hoping that she could get back there to join them.

In the base, the command said that it had been 'occupied', while the boys called it 'captured'. But whatever it was, the respite enjoyed by the boys was soon to come to an end. The official and commanders were meeting in the conference room, with TV cameras on them so that the boys could see clearly who they were.

Then Edward spoke into the microphone:

'Gentlemen, we hereby announce the seizure of this base and the missile control room. We draw your attention to the fact that any offensive from you will result in the buttons of the long-range missiles being pressed. As you can see, they are ready.'

On the TV sets the boys could see the commanders watching and the cameras were moved round the command console to make sure the situation was clear.

Those outside were waiting for those inside to reveal the identities of the 'attackers' as they were called. They had assumed that it had been one of the great superpowers that was responsible. Only such a power would have been able to understand the secret codes, which enabled the missiles to be launched.

It was time to speak out and then the high command was astonished and shocked when they saw that inside their command-room were three boys. Each of the boys stood in front of the camera and introduced himself, giving his name, his age.

Richard said, 'I am the leader, Edward the spokesman and Mark, technician.'

This was too much for one high-ranking officer. He could not control his anger. He shrieked, his face blazing with indignation, 'What is this nonsense? How could this have happened?'

Another officer shouted that they must stop being mocked in this way.

Richard broke in. 'Calm down, gentlemen! You must all accept the situation and listen to our demands. Don't forget that we can see you and hear you. If what we have heard is all you are going to say, we can set the world on fire in a few seconds!'

To their horror the officers saw the boys begin to set the command for the launch of the biggest long-range missile in the direction of the supreme super-power in the Eastern bloc. They saw the missile slowly emerging from its shelter.

'Stop it! Stop this destruction!' they screamed, now convinced that the boys were serious and had to be treated very carefully.

They soon realised they were part of the class that had visited the base the previous day. Questions were put to the officer that had let them in. who allowed it? Why were their numbers not counted and checked as they left? And more important, how did they know in such a short time how to operate the launching system and decode the ignition of the missiles?

Perhaps, thought the commanders, these boys are being supported by some other power and have been trained by an intelligence service for this operation. Meetings were held to see which officer was most suitable for conducting the negotiations. Hundreds of actions had to be taken.

But the boys' statement had not been completed and their demands had still not been made. There was nothing to do but wait, hear what the boys had to say. At the same time, many investigations were under way to try to find out who was helping them. It was unthinkable that they had acted by themselves.

Then Edward stood before the camera and said, 'We will soon deliver our main statement, but before that we must inform you of our essential demands in order to complete our peaceful mission. As soon as it is finished we will hand over the base and the control room and leave immediately.'

The commanders' spokesman nodded. 'Let's hear those demands. If all is right, we will do what we can to end the matter.'

Edward interrupted. 'The commanders should not act so hastily. We will make our demands when we are ready and every country must listen.'

He went on confidently. 'We must be allowed to talk to our parents. The press and other media must be given permission to follow what is being said. We want food sent up and official employees to be evacuated from the base.'

With a further warning about their determination to launch the missiles the statement ended: 'If any attempt is made to cut off the electricity we will immediately put the emergency generator into action and the missiles will be fired.'

Some objections were made about the presence of the press and TV, but the boys insisted, threatening to arm another missile to force the matter. Then they said that if all their demands were put into operation they would make their next statement at 4:00 p.m.

A last request puzzled the officials outside. The boys wanted the students who had been with them the day before to be allowed to join them. They did not understand the reason for it. But they sent in food, drink, and clothes, medicine-in amounts that seemed to indicate that the boys intended a long stay.

At the appointed time, TV cameras were switched on to show that the press and other media were present. Edward then spoke:

'Dear senior and other high ranking officers, we hereby address you and the whole world-including all peoples, countries, blocs Eastern and Western, and all international bodies.

We are a group of citizens of this great free country, whose fathers built it up by the shedding of their blood and through their sacrifice, so that we could live in peace and security. Such principles were designed to cover the whole world.

Our ancestors made this sacrifices-not so as to participate in the destruction of the world-on the contrary; their aim was that the world would live in freedom and peace. This is the principle of justice written in the Constitution of our country.

But we find that our country is moving with many other countries towards destruction. That it is soon to make the most killing mistake in all history.

The competition for the accumulation of destructive weapons is preparation for the destruction of the world-in seconds. There are mines and bombs in places all over the world. No one knows what they will blow up. Or who will be first to start the war.

Surely, all the millions of victims of classical weapons used in all the wars should be lesson enough to push the world toward peace? The world is not the place of peace and happiness described by our leaders. The world sits on top of a volcano about to burst. Who can stop it and save our world?

Gentlemen-this is what we are trying to stop universal destruction. The recent destructions in Chernobyl in the USSR are examples of the dangers threatening us. And there are short, medium and long-range missiles stationed all over the world, facing every direction. Any one can be launched by a hasty operation.

Don't forget-we were able to get in here and are free to launch massive and wide-spread destruction. This is how we see our lives, the official line about peace and security has no grounds in reality. We feel the world is moving towards more and more destruction. "ordinary" wars raging as the result of interference in other peoples' affairs.

We seek an exit out of this danger. This is why we have done what we have done.'

Edward stopped speaking, his pause leaving his silent listeners in suspense, wait-ing for him to continue. Could he convince the whole world that their mission was peaceful and not just a form of blackmail? It was important that they did not act carelessly and it was clear that the press was very surprised at the statement.

Then Edward spoke again:

'We are sorry gentlemen. We have to stop at this point until the rest of our party arrives from the camp. We began our statement in order to show our good inten-tions and the real nature of our mission.'

One of the officers outside spoke up. He said that they had been for but had not been found until troops caught up with their bus outside the city.

At first it seemed as if they were being accused of something, but then they were told that they were being taken to the base to join their friends.

The students talked privately to Mary about it, asking if they should go, and why.

Without hesitation, Mary told them yes.

'Your friends need your help, they are trying to compel the state to institute peace and security in the world and replace nuclear weapons. It is something we have discussed in school. Who among you wants to take part?'

Many students looked very puzzled and quickly Sarah stepped forward. 'I will go and I think you should all come with me!'

Sarah was held in great respect by the others and they all agreed except two. One was obviously very frightened and hesitating, the other seemed to be asleep.

They said goodbye to Mary and asked her to contact their parents and tell them that there had been no pressure on them to go to the base. Mary promised to go all the parents, as her class members got off the bus. A military vehicle was to take them to the base while Mary went back to visit each student's home.

When Mary saw the parents, most were shocked at the news and were very concerned for the safety of their boys and girls. Simon's father was anxious about the lad and Mary reassured him that none of the children would be convicted because they were all under age. When she spoke to Sarah's father he immediately went to see his lawyer, but was told exactly the same, that Sarah was too young to be convicted.

There were some who thought that their children had been wrong and it should not have been done. However, the situation was a fact and could not be changed. They all pleaded to see their children very soon. Mary answered that her pupils would not come to harm and the command would comply to all the demands. A few parents went straight to the base to see for themselves.

Some of the parents thought that Mary was the brains behind it all and the key figure, and on wanted to inform the authority but he was stopped by his wife. She reminded him of the sadness he had experienced when his brother was killed in another war. She said that the boys were doing something that no one else could do. 'Wait and see!' she insisted.

One father wanted to go to the police to report his missing son, but his daughter said that he had no grounds. Then he said he wanted everyone to know that his son was innocent and had not participated in any criminal action. It was obvious that he expected some kind of reward, for they gave details of Mary's role in what had happened. The result was that orders were given to bring Mary forward to hear what she had to say.

This news spread all over the country and people quickly gathered-something that was part of the plan.

In the city there was a lot of confusion, with police cars hurrying about, people were heading out of the base, the press was reporting everything they could.

In the base, the boys were told that their classmates had arrived. They instructed them to take over some of the key areas and learn how some of the operations were carried out. Others went on observation duty or made sure that the power was kept on. Some went to the kitchens and the clinic. Richard asked Sarah to show other students the way to the command-room were the three were.

The high command was frustrated on every side when they tried to find out what the boys were doing, and careful to keep their actions secret. Using their knowledge of the ventilation shafts, Sarah led five others into the control room. They were given observation and operational duties, replacing the three whom by now were very tired and had not rested since the previous day.

Mary continued to see parents and she was surprised at the different responses she received. There was anger, astonishment, and confusion.

At last she got back to her own home. She saw that David was awake. Sitting in his mobile electric chair, he had managed to switch on the TV to see what was going on. When he saw Mary he was delighted, he even tried to stand up and hold her but failed. He obviously knew that she had been involved in all the excitement at the base.

David was showing a remarkable recovery. 'David, it will come!' she said, stroking his hair. 'You will get your compensation. No, not in money or artificial legs-but in peace and comfort. The boys have to succeed when we get to the trail!'

Mary's pleasure was to be short-lived. She heard hard and loud knocking on the door and knew that behind that door was fear and trouble. But she was not frightened, she could rely on the boys who were carrying out the mission.

She opened the door to a man holding a CIA badge out. There were others behind him and they had clearly come to arrest her.

Very tired, she went without hesitation, knowing what was to come.

'May I call next door so that my neighbour can look after my husband?' she asked.

The man nodded and Mary bent over David and kissed him. Then closed the door behind her.

6

The country was in a state of shock. Everyone was talking about the group of boys, which had occupied the control room of a nuclear plant and demanded a trial. A trial of the world!

Little by little, news leaked through the media to all peoples. No state was able to keep the embarrassing fact a secret. The high command tried to obscure what was happening and hide some details, hoping to suggest that it was some kind of interference in military affairs. They put it out that it was a revenge operation, that the boys were just a bunch of teenagers led by a mentally sick boy still in shock from the death of his father while on duty.

Some commands did not take the matter seriously right from the beginning; they would deal with the boys in a way which would put an end to the situation before anything went wrong.

Outside the base, crowds were still gathering, their numbers increasing all the time. The spokesman for the forces took a jeep through the gate and tried to calm the shouting people. He turned to waiting reporters and groups of parents.

'Ladies and gentlemen! Let me explain what is happening! It is nothing but a boyish prank, a fruitless action by a group of youngsters trying to do the impossible! The got in but exploiting the friendly reception given by the personnel in the base to an official school visit, just like other visits. During these visits, many children play with controls and these boys did the same and it has become very unpleasant. We are trying to stop them with every means. We must be patient until they have been stopped.'

Many parents were pleading that they be allowed in to see their children. Reporters were trying to get more and more information about what was going on and camera teams bustled about to find the best vantage point.

The words of the officer in the jeep seemed to be calming the situation. He shouted, 'Believe me, it is nothing more than games which will soon come to an end!' Then he got back into the jeep and drove back into the base with the shouts of the crowd following him as mothers and fathers wanted to see for themselves what was being done.

From the control room, the boys calmly insisted again and again that nothing but a trial of the world would satisfy them. They must meet all the presidents and heads of state and negotiate for peace and justice. But these politicians were still taking the matter lightly.

There was meeting after meeting and many top-level arguments but there seemed no way but to accede to the boy's demands. The other students were brought in after pressure had been put on them not to help their colleagues.

Little by little the boys had their demands met. Once their friends were inside they said that all officers should be evacuated from the base and must leave all systems and instruments in working order.

There was opposition but it had no effect. All the boys would say was that there would be a peaceful end to the matter if their demands were met. The negotiations were short and soon the students were brought in.

They heard Richard's voice over the microphone. 'You are welcome to the base! This is where the trial of the world would take place, to proceed for peace. Friends are peace-makers and you will help establish justice throughout the world!'

'Fate decreed that we are all students in the same class. We studied the same subjects so we believe in the same principles. Please join us voluntarily. Anyone who feels that they are not acting willingly and legally can leave now!' there was a general agreement from the students at this.

One boy stood in front of the camera and said, 'We know what we are doing. It is what millions of people want. I speak for all my friends and myself when I say that we are standing with Richard and Mark and Edward. The leaders of the powers must be brought here together with their lawyers. Because charges will be made against them!'

Edward said that all communications would now stop until the morning. Then the doors to the guard hall would be opened to allow in those who had been requested to attend.

When the speakers fell quiet, those listening were still uncertain about the demands and whether they were peaceful or hostile. The way the boys had put their demands had convinced some, angered others who felt that these boys were a danger. Particularly now that they had been joined by the rest of the students, and had control over the whole base.

The command held a meeting to discuss the situation. The options were either to storm the base and get the three boys out, especially since all the entrances were not blocked. Or give in to the demands, which to many seemed perfectly reasonable if a trial were to be held.

Because the command was divided on the matter they tried to establish how they ought to react. Should they act democratically? But personal interests and benefits won and they finally decided that every party would do whatever they felt right. It was the only thing they agreed on. There was now arrangement that the boy's demands exhibited sound thinking. But it was a strange thing-the commands trusted the young people, but they did not trust themselves nor the leaders of any country in the world!

The boys in the control room were considered enemies and the command wanted to get rid of them one way or another, even by having them killed. But they hesitated because if the assault failed, the boys might launch the missiles, which would destroy large of the world and blame would fall at the feet of the command.

So, divided, the officers were in two groups, one preparing to use military force and storm the base during the night. The other to fulfill the boys' demands.

Bringing the world's leaders together was easy, as was organizing the judiciary and scientists of nations, which produced nuclear weapons. The one difficulty was in finding Mary. Groups searching for her failed to find her at home although she was reported as being there. Her husband was there, but he was not able to speak.

The officer in charge of the searching squads asked if she were at any police station or a security building. One thought she might be in hospital, he had noticed that she was very pregnant when he saw her in the girls' camp. So the group was divided into two, one to check with the police, the other to call at all the hospitals.

But Mary was in neither of those places. She was being held in a place where there was a security umbrella and had fainted under the pressure of severe interrogation. But after a few minutes she recovered consciousness and opened her eyes to see two or three intelligence officers standing round her.

She tried to sit up properly on the chair and asked them what they wanted. 'I have nothing to tell you! Please allow me to go home, I have told you all I know!' she whispered.

One man said, 'You haven't told it all because that would mean giving information about who it is that is behind this affair! How did you get these boys into the base?'

'Look, I swear to God,' muttered Mary, 'I've told you everything!'
he glared at Mary. 'Do you think that we are idiots to believe you're alone in this, for some weird motive?'

Mary could only nod her head, and one of the more kindly interrogators butted in. 'We don't want to harm you in any way or prolong this interrogation, Madam. But we must know which country is supporting you against us!'

The pressure got to Mary at this point and she burst into tears, sobbing that she had nothing more to tell them. 'Ask those boys, they will tell you!'

The questions began again, but differently, this was the 'soft' approach. She was offered a cigarette and refused it. 'I'm pregnant, can't you see that smoking would be harmful for my baby?' she snapped to the embarrassed agent.

The man tried again, 'We really don't want to harm you, all we want are facts,' he said, trying to be as nice as possible.

'For the hundredth time, I have nothing to do with any foreign country and I certainly not spying for an enemy!' she said.

But he held up his hand. 'We've heard it all before and we don't believe it! In some way you are involved with those boys out there in the base.'

'All right! Yes, I don't deny that. But believe it or not it is a peaceful mission and doesn't concern any state secrets. All we want to do is announce our objection to nuclear weapons-just as hundreds of other people do!'

The chief of the intelligence officers stiffened when he heard that, then he shouted, 'Do you call this the right way to object? Why not chose some other more peaceful way?'

But Mary could not give any more answers. She told herself that she must remain silent and they were obviously very annoyed by her new attitude.

One of them put it direct to her, 'You will be put under surveillance and all your movements will be followed. You will be arrested again and again and brought here for questioning.' His tone hardened then and he added menacingly, 'And if you were not pregnant we would have treated you very differently!'

Feeling ill and weak, Mary had fainted more than once. While she was held away from home and her handicapped husband for a whole day and night.

At home David was sick, yet he still had hope, he had seen it on Mary's face. From the day he had been brought home there was nothing left for him except hope. He could feel it in Mary's touch, her looks. But then came a moment when he suddenly felt a strange feeling in his body. It was the blood running through his veins. It was the first feeling of any kind since that terrible day when he was nearly killed.

That day was the unforgettable moment when Mary's students came to visit her before the visit to the base. It was the planning day and he remembered listening, seeing them talking, but unable to utter a single word. His thoughts went back to that day. He had seen their surprise when he tried to get closer to the table round which they were sitting. He had wanted to use his limbs, to stand up.

Mary saw this too and wanted dearly to help him, but she deliberately stopped herself. David himself had to make that great effort on his own. She forced herself to keep talking to the boys but her eyes kept slipping back to her husband. She raised her voice when she said that it was necessary to put an end to wars.

The boys had noticed that Mary seemed almost absentminded, and soon afterwards they realised what was happening. Suddenly, David was standing up-without help! The boys gasped and Mary ran round the table to put her arms round David and hug him.

David wanted to contribute to what was being said. He nodded his head towards the cabinet where he had kept military papers and information, even managing to move an arm slightly. There were words in his head, he tried but he could not turn them into words from his mouth. But it was such an unexpected improvement, everyone round that table cried tears of happiness.

Mary had been right when she decided that what he needed was some incentive to force him to improve his condition. It was nothing more than a miracle-he even tried to speak!

David remembered all this. He was not in his wheelchair behind the window, but resting his hands on the ledge. Then Margaret suddenly saw him and rushed round, horrified, not bothering to even knock before bursting in. He stood there, smiling, then reached out for his walking sticks and moved clumsily, haltingly toward her.

His voice was awkward, but just understandable. 'Please come in! Mary isn't home yet. I was standing by the window, hoping to see her coming,' is the gist of what he said.

Margaret stared at him. 'Are you all right?' she asked.

'Quite all right, thanks! But where's Mary? Where is she? When is she coming back?'

'Haven't you heard what is happening in that base outside the city?'
    David's voice went very quiet. 'Yes!' he whispered.
    'Well, Mary's students are behind that operation.'
    'Yes, I know,' he replied very distinctly.

Margaret was so happy to see such an astonishing change in David's condition. She asked, 'Is Mary involved too?'

David wanted to answer, but couldn't. He picked up his walking sticks and moved slowly into the living room. Margaret's intuitively knew that David wanted to be alone now, to sit and think about his wife. Where had she been all this time?

While this was happening in her home, Mary was in the CIA building being questioned, accused of being a spy for some foreign country.

She was rescued when the CIA received an order from military command, saying that Mary had to be brought to them at the base. It changed the strange situation in the interrogation room. They knew that they had been justified in arresting Mary, and now they really wanted to help her, to help remove the pain of that long, bitter interrogation. They knew that they were in big trouble and they asked Mary to forgive them. Coffee and food were brought, nothing was too much.

But Mary had seen films with scenes like this. She felt that it was probably just another trick-to lower her defences and make her sell freely. They apologized again, asking if they could do anything. All she could say was, 'I just want to go home and I want to see my doctor.'

They were standing in a corner now, talking quietly. One said, 'Do you think she is involved?' Another said, 'Look, we would willingly take you home, but we have had orders to take you back to the military base. So we have decided not to take you there until tomorrow so that you can get home get a good night's sleep and see your husband.'

Mary wanted nothing but to get home. The journey took but a few minutes and then she got out of the car and ran to the house.

David heard the car door slam. It just had to be her! He tried to get up from the settee where he had laid the whole of the long night.

Mary came into the room and saw David. Not able to speak, she staggered, then fell to the floor, just aware that he was struggling to reach her on his crippled legs.

She was crying when she recovered, with David clinging to her and murmuring, 'Oh! Mary, my love!' in his hoarse, hesitant voice.

He moved slowly, but time had stopped, it was not important. She had experienced a miracle, she had heard David talk and seen him move!

Mary had not realised that her plans, her work and especially her hardships could be the basis for cure for David. He dropped the crutches, he embraced her and they went into their bedroom to lie and embrace the night through, forgetting the world entirely, only aware that he had won his battle over his sickness.

While Mary and David slept in each other's arms there were many parts of the world which did not rest. It was now dawn, the dawn of the second day when a new sun was shining on the world, a sun that proclaimed peace and justice.

In the base, the students spent the night checking and working on their plans. They were now able to operate all the functions of the launching operations. The control room and the codes for firing the missiles were still under their control. The regular operators had been sent away and students were on guard everywhere. It had been for them a working night.

Dawn had just begun to give light to the sky now, and the young people holding the base were planning their next moves. The commanders were also busy, preparing to storm them, with suicide teams ready to penetrate the building through the ventilation ducts. They began worming their way along but their bodies were much larger than those of the boys. The smallest of the soldiers wriggled his way along and then his hand dislodged the walkie-talkie that Richard had left there. The others waited behind.

The sound of the small radio hitting the metallic floor of the duct alerted the students. Surely the command was not cheating, sending soldiers in to kill them? They had been promised that things were going smoothly. All those things that Edward had asked for had arrived.

Sarah and Richard went to investigate the reason for the noise while Simon and Edward continued their work on the surveillance system.

Minutes passed. All of a sudden a gas-bomb was thrown out of the entry to the vent! Then shouts rang out as a soldier fired shots into the control room where the boys were. Edward threw himself onto the floor, but Simon screamed as he was hit. He fell from the chair, bleeding, still just conscious, but dying.

The choking gas filled the air and Richard could see the canister on the floor with the gas hissing out. He bent down and picked it up, then threw it back into the vent where the soldier was hiding. The man saw it come back to him, touched it, then lost it again in the smoke and gas and panicked, falling limply as the gas reached his lungs.

He never saw the two boys who were standing there, guns in their hands and ready to shoot him the moment he came out of the duct.

It was not long before the commanders realised that the operation to storm the room had stopped. While the boys were subduing the soldier they looked round for Simon. The boy was trying to pull himself towards the control panel, but lost consciousness and fell on to one of the red buttons, red because it activated one of the missiles.

Simon began screaming then the boys saw that his head was resting on that button. They rushed over to move him but it was too late.

The missile had already been launched and was roaring up into the sky.

Richard picked up the microphone and said to everyone listening outside, 'your command has unsuccessfully tried to storm the room. We will go on with our plans. We are very sorry the command has acted in this way.'

Then he announced in a steady voice that a missile had been launched because of a soldier's action inside the control room, shooting at one of their group.

Richard followed with a warning. 'Do not take any more action to stop us! We ask you to prepare the trial as we instructed in our letter.'

Richard continued, 'Please move to the other hall with those who were invited to attend. Visiting students from all over the world will join our class to act as the jury, side by side with the judicial panel entrusted to make a judgement. We ask the judges to move to the stand so that all the procedures are perfectly legal. As in regular courts.'

One of the senior officers asked for some time to complete the arrangements, but Richard broke in, insisting, 'No break. The court must convene in one hour. You must call whoever you wish as witnesses and allow representatives of victims of the wars, peace and nuclear weapons control societies to be heard. Witnesses are needed, don't forget. And our teacher Mary must be found and brought here.'

The officers who had tried to make the attempt to storm the room now knew that their plan had failed. They had achieved nothing but the shooting and killing of one of the boys. Their faces showed disappointment and defeat. Their leader moved toward the TV cameras and announced, 'We agree to convene this trial, we have prepared ourselves, our president and all other presidents to get ready for the trial. Judges from every country have arrived to show our acceptance. We regret what has happened, it was done without the permission of the high command. We await your instructions.'

Everyone listening realised that this had not happened by chance, it had been very carefully planned. The previous night had been sufficient time for the three boys to make their plans, they had acted like experts. What puzzled everyone was who was behind it all?

Everyone called to attend the trial was shown his proper place. Then they waited for it to begin. Many felt a fear of what was to come. International personalities who had not come would think that they were about to witness some kind of aggression pact. But the group had shown their wisdom by inviting representatives from all the supreme powers.

The command felt as if they were sitting on a rumbling volcano about to erupt. It seemed to them that the boys' objectives were peaceful, so why all the hesitation? What could be more terrible than the launching of an uncontrolled missile? The latest reports they had were that it was moving slightly east-north-east. Where would it drop? What destruction would it cause?

The supreme commander of the army spoke to the students' leader as politely as he could. 'What are you waiting for? Everything is ready! Do you want to send up more missiles? We have agreed to begin, come on, start the trial!'

Richard's answer through Edward was that they had fulfilled all the requests except one. The cameras showed astonishment on the commander's face.

'As soon as that demand is fulfilled we will ask the accusing counsel to read the accusation out to the judicial panel and start the trial.'

'What is this request? What have we not done?' asked the commander. 'We have done all you ask!'

'No!' answered Edward. 'Our teacher Mary is not here, we cannot start the trial without her. She is our witness for the prosecution, she will give evidence against the accused!'

The commanders were in difficulty now, they prepared for a wait, but at what cost?

Urgent calls were made to get Mary and bring her to the base. But Mary refused to come. She said she was tired after the long interrogation in the CIA building and-more important-she was beginning to feel the delivery pains of her baby.

Outside Mary's house there were strange scenes. Army vehicles surrounded it as if she were a criminal under siege, wanted for justice.

She shouted for them to go away, 'I don't want to go with you!'

The officer in charge explained that he had orders to take her to the base, but Mary pointed to her husband, standing in the doorway with her, 'Look what you have done to my life!'

He said to her, 'But your pupils want you there!'

She felt more relaxed, but still refused the officer's request. 'How can I go there? look at my crippled husband!'

But David turned to her and said she should go in spite of his condition.

'And I am in labour pains now! What am I carrying, a live child or a dead one?'

At the officer understood that it was not reasonable to insist on taking Mary and he turned to leave.

But Mary caught his arm and spoke in a weak and tired voice. 'Please tell my class that I am with them and wish them success. Tell them that they must persevere without harming anyone. And tell your high command whatever you want about me!'

This brought a feeling of compassion for Mary. Although weak she seemed strong and the officer wanted to tell his superiors about Mary's reaction even though he had no right to. He removed his cap and spoke quietly to her.

'I will inform the high command nothing but what I have seen here, that you just cannot come because of your health. As for your students, I cannot tell them directly but they will know through our communication system. Please accept my apologies for our actions!' Then he saluted and went back to his car and was driven back to the base, where he made his report.

At the base, the commander faced the camera linking him to the boys. He spoke carefully. 'I beg you to start the trial, your teacher Mary cannot come because she is in childbirth at the hospital.'

His statement seemed sincere and Mark said they should accept what he said.

Their answer came back, 'We believe you. We had to be sure that she is well, and we will now start the trial. In a few minutes we will send our legal representative to read the accusation charge and discuss the evidence. We will prove to the jury the soundness of our acts and confirm the mistakes made by the high command.'

They asked that all entrances to the court should be locked until the trial was over.

This was the crucial moment for the world. Everybody in the hall was holding their breath. It was very quiet.

Suddenly the outer door was flung open and an officer ran in. he stopped before the commander, gasping for breath, and saluted him before handing him a message. The commander read it and addressed everyone.

'We are safe this time! The missile landed in a thinly populated area of the far north. No one was hurt and no damage done. Let us hope that nothing like this will happen again!'

He turned to the camera, which linked him to the three boys. They had heard what he said and said they were happy and relieved. They too hoped that it would not happen again, and asked that all information about casualties and damage would be passed to them.

'Now let us begin the trial!'

7

Throughout the world it is the practice that judiciary council members, lawyers, the jury, all involved on the case and any members of the public should be present in court before the presiding judge enters the courtroom. It is then that the trial can begin. But this time the counsel for the prosecution was late and because of this the trial had to be delayed.

Everyone else had arrived and taken their seats. They understood their roles and were very much aware of the gravity of the case. A reckless act by the command had caused dreadful destruction, and it had thankfully not hit any thickly populated area. No there was no room for ill-considered action-giving a second chance for another nuclear missile to be launched.

The trial might well be held at the expense of the leaders' arrogance. It could expose their faults and corrupt policies. Was that wrong? Would it not be a good thing, good for mankind? This was the reasoning behind it made by everyone in the court, although it was a daring thing to do. Everyone thought back to the events leading to the trial, and they evaluated the options open to them. These thoughts reassured all those there that setting the trial up had been a sound decision.

The silence was broken by the sound of the door opening separating the courtroom from the judge's chamber. The people stood, looking towards the open door to see who was coming in. who could it be? Surely it was some great presence, it would be the voice of the students, of justice, of peace. It would be the representative of thousands of millions of people, all mankind! The counsel for the prosecution.

But they saw no one. In disbelief, the standing people turned to each other and wondered. The open door was then pulled shut as if there was some reluctance.

Sarah had hesitated before the open door. She wanted to hide her inward timidity, while the people who knew her were aware of her courage and resolution. The pause had enabled her to regain her composure. Followed by the judge, she then walked through the door into the courtroom and into the witness-box. And the people applauded her, clapping and cheering until the judge pounded the bench with his gavel, demanding order and quiet until the court settled down.

The last group to be quiet were the world's celebrities who had been summoned as former rulers of the super-powers. They now sat with questioning eyes, staring round and scanning the courtroom in fear, a fear aggravated by the sight of the young counsel for the prosecution. Sarah sat down as the judge finally quieted the courtroom, but she was exhausted.

The presiding judge announced the beginning of the trial.

'Today, the trial of the heads of state before you begins. They have been brought here in accordance with prior agreement and pledges made between the students and the leaders of the world present here.'

'On these grounds, this trial is being held legally and officially. The decision of the court, however, will come from members of the jury sitting before you and who are students elected from countries in the world related and concerned with this subject. Taking their decision into account, this judiciary council formed from a number of super-powers, will pronounce their verdict either of conviction or acquittal. These proceedings will be, first, listening to the charges brought, the points of view of the prosecution, and the defence of the accused.'

There was a gasp from the public at the use of the word 'accused' and the judge again had to call for silence. Then he continued, 'It should not e surprising to describe the world's leaders present here as the accused. All possible measures have been taken to hold this trial in the most decent manner so that right will prevail. We have taken an oath to that effect. We will discharge our duties until there is a fair and just conclusion.

The executory measures of the verdict will be left to the higher authorities who arranged these proceedings. We tell the students in the control room that it will be carried out, it is what we have promised to do under oath and we shall do so.'

Three boys in particular watching by the means of TV cameras were happy at what the judge had said. They wanted to stand up and cheer, but they restrained themselves. This was only the first victory, the mission was not over, the battle had not yet been won.

It was Edward who said, 'We've just got to wait and see, we haven't won yet, so be prepared for surprises!'

But Richard was deep in thought, he was not taking as much interest in what was happening as the other two.

'What's the matter?' Edward asked him. 'You look bemused.'

Richard shook his head, 'I'm all right, but I am concerned about our teacher Mary. Where is she? Is she well? Has she had her baby yet? If only she were here with us to share this moment of triumph. After all, she was the one who started it all!'

'You're right, Richard, we'll finish today what we have started and then go tell her all about it,' said Edward.

'Come on, then, let's call up the student groups,' said Richard, and he watched Edward using his expertise to talk to the students outside, where they were working under his command and dealing with the base personnel.

First, Richard wanted to talk to the base doctor to find out how Simon was, the boy who had been shot and severely wounded when the soldier had fired from the ventilation duct into the control room. He also asked about the same soldier, because he had been a victim of the gas that had been used ineffectually against them.

He was told that both he and Simon had been rushed to hospital.

The doctor's report was anything but encouraging, Simon's bullet wound on his head had put him in a serious condition. There was fear that he might die unless his constitution was strong enough for him to hold on. He needed surgery and top surgeons were due to be arriving soon.

'What about the soldier?' asked Richard, and was told that the man was still suffering from the effects of the gas and was seriously ill. He thanked the doctor and asked to be kept informed of any change in the patients' conditions.

Richard then spoke to another part of the base, enquiring on the progress of the work there, and was told that things were in order. The trial, he was told, was being conducted in a controlled and proper way. Now he could relax. He leant back in his chair in the control room, sad the only person he could not talk to was Mary.

At that moment Mary was lying anaesthetized in the hospital's operating theater. Her labour pains were becoming horrendous and when she was examined it was found that her baby was not lying in the correct position but traversed across her womb.

The doctors were puzzled about this but they were aware of the traumas and tensions that Mary had suffered. This mispositioning of the foetus was not unusual of course, but X-rays showed that it had the umbilical cord round its neck and had turned sideways. If her condition had not been discovered soon enough, it was likely that she would have died with her baby unborn.

On the operating table, Mary did not know how serious her condition was, her thoughts had long been concentrated on the great trial which was now under way. She had collapsed on the floor of her home after the CIA search party had left, her labour pains increasing and there was a haemorrhage too.

When Mary had cried out in agony, David stumbled and struggled as fast as he could to Margaret and Bernard's door. When it opened under his knocking his neighbours found it difficult to comprehend what the frightened David was trying to say. His words were barely understandable but Bernard quickly saw that Mary was in trouble and rushed over to her while Margaret called an ambulance.

Just before she was away, Mary's thoughts turned to the miracle of her husband's part recovery. He was slowly beginning to regain his health and mobility, plus the possibility that he might soon be able to talk a little. It seemed to Mary as if it were a corpse returning to life.

She lay on the stretcher in pain as the ambulance drove at speed to the hospital. The pain was a warning to her from her body and she knew something was wrong. Her eyes were fixed on David, who had insisted on going with her, and he sat by her side.

Then Margaret looked at Bernard who was sitting on the other side. 'Please!' she gasped. 'If I die please take care of my baby…we want to call it Peace.' Her voice died away as she slipped into unconsciousness.

David, drawn and worried, clumsily patted her hand, murmuring, 'Please, Bernard, will she make it?'

Their doctor friend checked Mary's pulse and finding it weak noticed how thin she was.

He looked at David. 'I hope so,' he said.

In the hospital, Mary's evidentially serious condition brought a team of doctors hurrying to her. It was decided that at whatever cost her baby must be saved. It looked very much as if her condition was so poor that she would not be strong enough to hold out. But the baby did have a chance of survival.

Just as Doctor James was lifting the baby from Mary's wracked body he saw that the cardiograph recording her heartbeat showed a single, unwavering line instead of the regular pulsing of a living organ.

Mary would never see her child, or the child its mother. Never would it crawl toward her, or hold its arms out to be picked up and comforted when it cried. Mary was now mother to thousands of children round the world. Responsible for them, the cause of their survival but would never know them or see them.

She had sacrificed her life for her cause but had given the world her successor who would immortalize her memory. Mary had also left behind her husband David, who would tell her story to forthcoming generations.

There had been no pain in Mary's death and her life, though short, had been one of struggle, of epic deeds in the cause of peace for all generations to come.

Richard was looking out of a window and he suddenly saw a flock of birds circling the base. Then one bird, a brilliant white dove with rays of light glancing from it wings, perched on the sill of the window. It was followed by other doves flying up and landing by the first dove on a window of the courtroom. The arrival of the dove was not a coincidence. It had a significant impact on the students and gave them the extra strength to press on with resolve and determination.

The arrival of the doves coincided with the final words of the judge's opening sentences concerning the proceedings of the trial. Everyone had seen the dove's gleaming wings fluttering as it landed on the windowsill. It was seen as a good omen. Perhaps that the world's other inhabitants had sent their representative to witness the trial, knowing somehow that they, too, were victims of the same deadly weapons.

But the judge had finished his opening statement. He gave the floor to Sarah, counsel for the prosecution, who stood by the table accompanied by an attorney, the eminent lawyer appointed to the trial by an organization for the preservation of peace and the campaign for nuclear disarmament. He had himself for petitioned for the court's permission to allow him to aid the students. His first concern was to uphold the law and to counsel the students on legal details.

At first, Sarah felt it nearly impossible to speak in the atmosphere of the courtroom, packed with people staring at her. She felt scared stiff. On the table before her were a scatter of papers and the notes she had prepared. At her side her counsel patted her hand to raise her morale and whispered encouragingly, 'Be brave! Be brave! You can do it!'

Sarah glanced at the cameras through which her companions in the control room were watching her. She recalled everything that had happened. The soldier in the vent, the shots, Simon being hit and bleeding as he fell. She felt strength flood into her and she began to speak, looking at the accused.

'You were quite happy when the nuclear rocket fell harmlessly onto a distant Northern region. You never thought about the destruction caused by the missile, which could have killed a large number of people. It did not cause you any grief for the young men who gave their lives to uphold truth in a fair trial. Simon might have sacrificed his life in a cause against tyranny, whose intransigence could have blown up the whole world.'

Sarah then addressed the whole courtroom. 'Will you all stand for a minute's silence and pray for Simon's life or mourn his death and the souls of millions of innocent people who have been the victims of the world's crimes?' She paused and was pleased when she saw them come to their feet quietly, their heads bowed.

In her efforts to invoke guilt and remorse, Sarah's aims were clear. For everyone realised that she was trying to expose the errors committed by the world's leaders, their responsibility for the mad arms race and the proliferation of nuclear weapons. There was an irresponsible competition in their production while multilateral threats were imposed by the super-powers on each other.

'It can only end in horror and terrifying, deadly fear-and it could at any moment become real!' she cried. 'Nuclear weapons have been produced which can be used when the right opportunity arises; we are told that their use is prevented by wisdom, reason, logic and that is how it should be. Humanity comes first, before bias, racial prejudice, colour and regional origin. Now, every day this warring world muddles along with its problems.'

She was becoming used to it now, continuing, 'What prevents the use of these weapons should not be because they are available in large numbers. World power should not strike a balance and keep the peace that way. It is not true justice. The scales of the balance cannot be loaded with explosives as well as discretion, reason, reconciliation and understanding!'

Sarah's eyes were fixed on the jury now. 'Members of the jury!' she said, and she turned to the judge. 'Your Honour,' she added. 'There must be a way of meeting the world's problems, of bringing reality to our calls for peace rather than the repeated official slogans extolling world peace!'

'There have been slogans all over the world which have misled us; our rules have glorified these so-called peace slogans. But they are fakes. Used to impose power and authority, to justify the hoarding and deployment of lethal weapons. Leaders have used the phrase Balance of Power as an excuse for the accumulation of more an more weapons of destruction. It seems not to occur to them that at any time their bluff may be called. A mistake during practice, an impulsive drive by one side against another in this frenzied search for profit, self-interest and domination.'

'All this has been done by the leaders brought into this courtroom in the name of justice. We have deliberately sought the rule of justice they have so often inflicted, without any consideration for the people's safety and security.'

'This has been our motive. We have jeopardised our lives for it. We mean no evil to those brought here. But we really believe that if things stood as they are much longer the world would eventually and inevitably explode in a nuclear holocaust. All the signs are there.'

'We are told that life is progressing, developing, manufacturing, becoming better. In reality it is moving toward the abyss, a trap. There will be a frantic rush to be the power with the most strength, the power that will never be second to another.'

'For what other reason is the increasingly destructive power of nuclear weapons? It is like an epidemic, a spread of some terrible disease. So is there an excuse? I ask the leaders of the world present here for their answers, their testimony in their defence.'

Sarah paused. 'I will stop at this point, but reserve my right to continue with the prosecution statement and cross-examination after listening to the defendants and their witnesses. These are fair demands and are in accordance with the rules and procedures of the honoury judiciary court, mutually agreed to before convening this trial and according to the terms of the memorandum of understanding drawn up specially for the purpose.'

'To end this part of the speech for the prosecution I cannot forget the gratitude and proper respect due to the judiciary council, the jury and all the defending world leaders present in this courtroom. At the same time we respect and uphold their right to their leadership of the super-powers. Nonetheless, we expect to be told about the plans apropos nuclear armament, barring any discussion of political issues regarding which the leaders may be right in withholding. We have no views on such issues. Nor are these issues subject to litigation in this court today.'

'I wish to thank the learned defence counselors as well as my learned colleagues for their invaluable help which enabled me to make this brief opening statement. Thank you all for listening.'

As soon as Sarah stopped speaking everyone in the court rose to give her a standing ovation. It astonished the judge so much that he failed at first to hammer with his gavel on the bench to demand silence. He and the other members of the council had never heard anything like it in a court of law.

But it was like any previous court of law. The world's leaders and rulers were being prosecuted. The world's leaders and rulers were being prosecuted and their renowned counsellors found themselves acting as defendants in a highly doubtful case. How could they stand against a prosecution which had a case that needed so little evidence? That young girl was capable of winning an impressive acclamation from the whole court as well as those listening in or watching the trial on the television.

'What are we going to say?' asked the defence lawyers. 'What evidence are we going to produce to prove our leader's innocence?'

One said that they should stage the best defence possible then leave the verdict up to the court even if it were a guilty one. And he looked at the heads of state sitting next to them.

The storm of applause for Sarah had died down. But there was a small group who would not stop talking and their interruption prohibited the court from continuing its work. The judge was determined that he would maintain silence and ordered the court bailiff to stop people making the noise or he would have them removed from the court. Guards were called and their appearance and the necessary effect, for the disturbance quickly stopped.

Sarah looked at the TV cameras and microphones, wondering what her companions in the control room had so far thought of her performance and whether they felt she was able to contribute enough to bring the trial to its proper conclusion.

8

In the control-room Saraha's friends were much more than satisfied. They were overjoyed with Sarah's work. While she was speaking they had been clapping and jumping up and down on their chairs in total admiration of the girl's prosecution speech.

Now that the courtroom was quiet again the judge called Sarah but she did not respond. Her name was called twice more and the people were beginning to wonder is something were wrong. Suddenly the girl realised that her name was being spoken and she jumped to her feet and faced the judge, who asked her if she had anything else to say before hearing the defence.

"Thank you, Your Honour, I'm sorry I did not hear you. I would like to listen to the statement of the counsel for the defence and afterwards make my comments on it, 'she said.

The judge looked over to the table where the defence conusellors representing the heads of state sat. "Will the defence now present its reply to the prosecution's statement? He asked.

But the defence lawyers sat motionless. Probably, for the first time in their professional lives they were baffled, speechless. One of them everyone here for the students is overwhelming. I wonder if my colleague feels the same way.

So the judge tried again. He looked at the defence table sand remained them that it was their turn to stand and address the court. 'Will the counsellor make the defence statement? Otherwise the court will move on to calling witnesses'.

He simply had to say something, so the defence lawyer hurriedly got to his feet. 'Justice is undoubtedly an important matter and a requirement for every aspect of life. It is no doubt the thing everyone seeks. Here, a gang of students in this country have embarked on a provocative and suicidal act in order to blackmail the state and exert pressure for conveing this court'.

He would have continued, but immediately there was concern on the defence's table and the prosecution's legal adviser whispered urgently to Sarah.

She rose and spoke. 'Your Honour', she said, 'I object to my learned colleague's use of the expression "provocative and suicidal". She added that it was a point which had been settled and a memorandum of agreement had been signed by both parties.

The judge considered the objection and conceded that it had been agreed before hand. But he felt that the defence could describe matters as he saw them. The court would decide, he said, and invited the defence lawyer to continue.

The defence said, 'If the memorandum of agreement gave some temporary legitimacy to the trial, or if it was the result of pressure and coercion this would nullify the trial...

It was again obvious that the people in the court did not agree. However, Sarah did not object, letting the man continue,'...and that these proceedings according to t e memorandum do not aim at chastising these esteemed gentlemen before you, the world's leaders'.

Again, the public in the court interrupted, their cries of dismay echoing round the court as they herd the excessive terms of praise for the heads of state. Three loud bangs of the gavel rang out and quietened the court, allowing the defence once again to continue.

"The objective of the court must be neither punishment nor reward for there has been no action that deserves punishment and consequently this trial is groundless and should be ruled null and void, 'said the defence.

This time Sarah did not consult her learned colleagues, but stood up. "May I object again, Your Honour? She said. 'How can the defence call this trial groundless and void, when he and the heads of state cooperated raising the memorandum of agreement and put their signatures to it?

For the second time the judge agreed with Sarah and found her objection reasonable, He spoke to the defence counsel, "Will both counsels please approach the bench'.

The defence were obviously un comfortable about this but rose and went to stand before the judge, with Sarah standing beside them, It looked incongruous, the small figure of the girl beside the two large men.

The judge peered down at the girl with some sympathy. As for Sarah, she felt that while the efence counsel were tall and she small, in terms of rights and position she stood on an equal footing. She was the 'wise old man' of her grandfather's generation.

The judges, too, she knew, accepted her as an equal before them, even though the two defence counsel stood above the bench while she was hardly visible. In fact, the judge had to stand and lean over the bench before he could see her, even though she was on her toes. Had the matter been not so important it could have been amusing and the public stifled their laughs.

Then the judge spoke to the prosecution and defence. "there is no need to raise the issue of the legitimacy of this litigation. You must both realise that your agreement was binding upon you.

As for ruling out punishment, it was agreed to on the presumption that the whole affair is peaceful in to and the objective is in bringing evidence, hearing the truth and dispensing justice. These are the terms of the memorandum, so return to your seats and adhere to those terms'.

Thanking the judge, both prosecution and defence went back to their tables and sat down.

Now, the defence continued with its statement. 'Without going into the bases and roots of this trial, the defence must make it perfectly clear that these leaders and heads of state have consented to come here and be party to the trial out of their humanitarian concern and their belief in working for the cause of mankind.

'As the world is aware, they have great duties and responsibilities which keep them very busy, so busy that they should not be here. However, they realised that it was part of their duty to participate in order to put an end to the senseless and serious mistake committed by the plaintiffs.

'As everyone knows, they are nothing but a handful of students taking advantage of the state's good nature and leniency. They infiltrated the heart of the nuclear base and took control of the equipment, putting it into operation for their purpose.

'The students do not realise how dangerous this can be, it can lead to a world catastrophe. In fact, this might have occurred had there not been some divine intervention when an intercontinental missile fell on a northern, sparsely populated region.

'Nevertheless, its destructive effects are still spreading to wider and wider neighbouring areas. Why? Because these young people claim wider neighbouring areas. why? Because these young people claim that they are seeking justice through this court!

'If there is any danger, they have brought it tot he surface and used it to threaten humanity. Remember, before these youngsters committed their abominable act this weapon was lying safe in its bunker. Solely to be launched and controlled by these great men with their wisdom and intelligent leadership. What is the danger claimed by these youngsters? It is no more than an unfounded fear on their part. The danger is unlikely to occur as long as we are ruled and governed by our brilliant leaders!'

The defence silently pointed to the heads of state sitting in the dock. He started at the, then continued in a subdued voice, 'the whole point hinges on the heads of state and their management. All we need to do is place ourselves in their hands and trust them.

He paused yet again, then hesitated and his words stumble, '…but…' until the judge demanded that he carry on. Still the defence counsel mumbled, repeating one word, 'But…'

He started at the heads of state, trying to collect his thoughts, then his eyes dropped to the floor until he was severely prompted by the judge to continue.

Raisin his eyes to the judge, the counsel for the defence blurted out, 'But….but they are only human, human! I cannot say any more,'

He looked tired, exhaustion showed on his face, then he stared at the heads of state and repeated 'Yes, humans. They are human beings and are in control of the world. One order from them, one finger on the buton…I am aware of the psychology of all people young and old, sesible or foolish…'

He looked desperate now. He said quietly, 'May I be excused form continuing? I feel exhausted and request that my colleague takes over.'

His colleagues saw that the burden of the defence had passed to him He knew why his colleague had stepped down after his enthusiasm had gone. He had introduced a dangerous qualification for the defenc at an inopportune moment. It was right that he stopped when he did because the gist of the statement would have changed and taken another course. Everyone in the court understood it, making them feel sorry for the lawyer.

The defence had failed to exonerate them; it had come into collision with a truth that humans have specific traits, some of which are not dependable. And they are capable of stockpiling horrendous numbers of weapons which could annihilate everything.

The court understood that the defendants were human beings, that in their hands lay the reins of world security and safety. But these aspirations could not be guaranteed by human beings. Only by God the only source capable of controlling these standards. Humanity will continue to be undependable, not to be trusted with momentous matters. It was clear, as clear as if it had between written on the wall of the courtroom.

The defence still lay in the hands of the second consel. He was expected to do his job as best he could. His colleagues had trapped him in a complex situation, a maze. He knew, too, that it was the business of lawyers to extricate their defendant's unscathed form such a maze.

They should be capable of disentangling themselves out of legal problems. So he stood up and tried to compensate for their failure so far. Could he continue the struggle begin by his colleague, but which had ended-and still hung in the air-'But they are human!'.

He walked toward the bench and approached the jury, stopped and glanced at his notes. What else could he say now that the whole thing was clear? What could he add? Boldly, he said that yes the leaders were human. But did that rule out their ability to invent things which might protect them from the dangers of the human intellect.

'Yes!' he said. 'We admit that we are human, we are not fods. If human beings seek to produce weapons and to arm themselves, counter-forces will emerge so that no single power may be left in control of the world. Any power can neutral-lise any other, raise a force equal to any other and so create a balance in the world. But it had led to the prolliferation of nuclear weapons, the subject of this trial.

'However, if we still believe that the human intellect is un reliable and that it is prone to emotion and change-and I can see it in your eyes-then we must be can-did and admit that fear of the human intellect was the motive for this trial. Nuclear power should not be left in the hands of a single human being, one heads of state. Guarantees must be made by all parliaments and elected groups of the public. Decisions should be made this way'.

Sarah could not control her impatience or remain silent any longer. She rose and requested the judge's permission to comment. The eyes of the court turned to her and then her colleague pulled at her hand and she realised that she had made her move at the wrong moment. She allowed him to pull her back into her seat and whisper to her. The judge quietly smiled his toleration and motioned to her, "You will have the right to make your comment after the defence counsel had financed his statement and discussion,' he said.

But Sarah's inopportune intervention had placed her in the hands of the defence. At this point the defence said that their witnesses could be called for cross-exami-nation.

Turning to Sarah, the judge said that it was her turn now. "You may now cross-examine any of the defence witnesses'.

She thanked him and began to speak. "This tiring trial must be as short as possi-ble and an end made t the tension apparent in all our faces, I would like to tell all members of the public and Outside observers that we are determined to press on with our claims. Our main objective remains in the proof that the faults of the world are represented by super-powers. Their deadly habit of engaging in fren-zied and irresponsible competition in the proliferation of nuclear weapons and in their threats to use them.

'All we ask is to have the arms ace labelled an error. Then let justice make its deci-sion. When this is done the world can see the avoidance of an an imminent trag-edy by destroying all nuclear weapons before they destroy us.

'the prosecution therefore requests permission to listen to some witnesses, beginning with the commander-in-chief of one of the two major Western military alliances then with their opposite number from the Eastern bloc'.

Sarah found it difficult to conceal her apprehension. In spite of the bravado she had shown since the trial had began, she was not professionally trained in law, not even an amateur in the matter of litigation. She had to rely on her strong belief in the justice of the case.

After a short consultation with her legal colleague, she approached the judge and asked that one of her associates be allowed to assist her, the enormous responsibility was great and she was tiring.

The judge gave his assent and Sarah returned to her table. Using a walkie-talkie she spoke quietly into it while standing in front of the TV cameras. After a moment a man appeared in the doorway of the courtroom, walked to the prosecution's table and sat down. Nobody knew who he was.

Then the commander-in-chief of the alliance was called in and he sat down in the witness-box. The judge waited for Sarah to speak, but she was still consulting with her adviser and taking notes.

Everyone was with her, the public in the courtroom and the millions outside, watching and listening. There were some who were frightened and apprehensive, even saddened about the prospects of a doomed world. It was matters like these that Sarah discussed as she sat at the table. At last she gathered her notes and stood up, before walking towards the man in the witness-box.

He was an old man in his late sixties or seventies but his military background gave him a firmness. And he had a presence in his uniform with its insignia and medals. None of this could affect Sarah and she put her first question.

'Sir, you are a commander-in-chief of the greatest alliance in the world. Will you please tell the court which countries recognise this alliance.

Without hesitation and with a look of pity, the man said that the question and its objective were obvious. The prosecution wanted to accuse those countries and their leaders who were in court without having to question them. He named the countries and their leaders and at each one Sarah stopped and stared.

Again, Sarah spoke to the general, 'In your capacity as an official representative of the alliance, can you talk about the military policy of the alliance?

'Yes!' answered the man, without hesitation, looking confident. 'We know that our policy is a composite of the policies of the member countries. This is right and it is effective to the system which is unique to the alliance.

Sarah said that they should get into the subject. Did the alliance approve of the policies of deploying nuclear weapons on the soil of member countries and how did it take place?.

The reply was that it operated according to a plan endorsed by the member countries and all were bound by that plan. Sarah wanted to prove to him that she and all the world knew about the plan and there was no sense in concealing any aspect of it or being ashamed mentioning certain facts.

She said, 'Member countries in cooperation with the alliance or without it have deployed hundreds of nuclear missiles on their soil aimed at vital areas in cities of the other bloc. This bloc had a similar alliance. 'She then exhibited figures and statistics and read them out to the court, passing the man a copy.

He was angry now, finding himself disparaged and denigrated by a young girl who was trying to expose his conscience and the humanity in him. He interrupted her as she spoke, his voice resentful, 'so what is wrong with all that?' It was a rhetorical question and was seen as such.

Sarah said, 'You ask what is wrong? We want an answer. It is the matter underlying these proceedings. You do not know, do not realise what is wrong with your plan. It is only something the public knows is wrong. The leaders cannot see it as wrong!'

Sarah realised that there was a weak link in the testimony, but it must be used at a later date, so she addressed the judge, saying, 'Your Honour, I would like to recall this witness after listening to the testimonies of other witnesses.'

Permission was given and it was pointed out that the witness could be recalled on condition that the defence had the right to cross-examine. The judge asked, 'does the defence wish to cross-examine?'

A defence lawyer answered, 'Your Honour, we have no objection to recalling the witness. We yield the right to cross-examine. 'the witness was then dismissed and he rose and walked to his seat obviously tense and worried, looking like a man waking up after a terrifying nightmare while the judge looked approvingly at Sarah.

Sarah spoke, 'Your honour, I have a list of names of people I would like to appear before you. There is no need to cross examine any of them, their presence will suffice.' She produced the list and began calling out the names of the victims, first from Japan.

9

'Kaifoyama Shita-Hiroshima…
Toshiki Moriyama-Hiroshima…
Tokoyo Nakayama-Nagasaki…'

As their names were called, one by one they walked towards the front of the courtroom. They looked old, not simply through years but because of the scars on their faces and hands. One was just able to walk, another was learning on his shoulder, the third was in a wheelchair being pushed by an orderly. It was a sight very painful to all those viewing it. Everyone was touched, moved and saddened. These were the witnesses of nuclear war.

Then Sarah read out her next list of names:

'Varna Polokov…
Vladimir Siryasky…'

Both were so crippled and deformed they had to be helped.

'These two people are enough. They are the victims of an unintentional accident at the nuclear reactor, the one at Chenobyl, claimed to be for peaceful purposes. But remember the destruction it caused.'

Sarah had not finished her list of 'witnesses'. She read out a third group of names from Vietnam.

'This woman and student have appealed to me not to give their names for special reasons.'

They were brought to the front.

The defence lawyer rose and objected to the parading of witnesses in such an emotion-raising way.

'I object, Your Honour, to this theatrical style, it will only appeal to the emotion of the masses, the jury, the judges..!'

Sarah stood up quickly, saying that she had made the point of the parade clear. 'And may I remind my learned colleagues that I gave up my right to question them in order to save the time of the court and consider it sufficient to show them in person to the court.'

It seemed as if the judge was hypnotised by the sight of the witnesses. He did not acknowledge Sarah's comment, he simply motioned to the lawyer and murmured quietly, 'Overruled!'

So Sarah resumed her list of witnesses from the USA.

'Mr James Parker…
Mr Michael Jefferson…
Mrs Helen Arthur…'

Two men came forward, crippled, one leaning on crutches, the other on a wheel-chair, totally maimed. Sarah did not explain how they received these injuries except to say that they were as a result of war. But the woman did not show any visible injury, so why was she there?

Sarah felt impelled to explain. 'Mrs. Arthur was not in Vietnam, or any other war involving the USA. But as a citizen, an army officer's widow, she is typical of thousands of women. Her husband spent his life in the army and died in Viet-nam. This woman, once a faithful wife but now a widow is also a prostitute. She was subjected to blackmail and harassment by officials after her husband's death. She found herself crushed under all the pressures and finally had no other choice but to become a prostitute, forced into it by society. Now she suffers from physi-cal and psychological troubles. She is addicted to drugs and gets them by any means. She came to this court as a sample of a social group created by war. She is only one of many.'

As Sarah was talking about her the woman was crying. The public responded and felt sad, bitter at the things war can do. They looked over to the world's leaders with hate in their eyes.

This was not lost on the judge, the atmosphere was highly charged and to avert any trouble he asked Sarah if she were finished with this parade of witnesses. But she had not yet finished, asking that she be permitted to produce two more groups.

Privately, the judge was interested in seeing more witnesses, which seemed to be convincing evidence for Sarah's cause. He felt that she had done enough but was bound to give all parties equal chances for questioning, so allowed the request.

Holding another list, Sarah called out more names, these from the Middle East:

'Khaleel Abdulrahman Abushamah-Palestine…
Elias Aboud Elhaji-Lebanon…
Waheed Aldeen Muhammad Na'eem-Afghanistan…'

And Sarah added that she had many others from other countries in the Middle East and other regions.

Now the judge interrupted, 'I think these present are enough.'

The witnesses are in a sorry state, the Afghan still bandaged, the Palestinian laying on a stretcher, his remaining hand raised in a victory sign, typical of his people, while the Lebanese was one-legged.

Sarah wanted to comment on the victims as they appeared, and was waiting for the chance. It was provided for her by the defence lawyer.

He shouted; 'Your Honour, these injuries especially the last ones, have nothing to do with the subject of this case. They were not sustained in a nuclear war or as a result of the nuclear industry. Moreover the hands of state before you were not part of any of the wars, which were internal, civil wars involving local governments and their citizens. I protest against this kind of testimony. And more that the court strikes them from the case records.'

The judge listened to the objection, understood its goal and seemed to find it valid. He turned to Sarah and her colleague to see if she would make some form of reply. But she was preoccupied, too involved to notice the judge looking toward her.

'What do you have to say to this? You heard them!'

Sarah realised that the judge was asking her if she had any comments. She wanted to be specific but found herself in an awkward position. Of course, she did not want that testimony to be struck from the record, so she said, 'Please, one minute! One minute, Your Honour!'

The judge stared at Sarah. 'One minute for what? What is your response? Have you a reply?'

'Yes. But I want to present it in figures and documents. They are ready but we do not have them here.' Sarah said this reluctantly, then asked if she might be relieved by her associate, and permission was granted.

Sarah's associate stood up and spoke, 'I was hoping to respond to the learned defence counsel's objection by producing official statistics that have been made public. I have foreseen the matter and have brought this evidence with me. But at no time did I expect the defence to resort to self-contradiction in order simply to raise objections. Is the claim to establish a matter of fact by implying that the super-powers are not involved Middle-East conflicts and wars?'

He paused. 'Despite the official figures and statements from the super-powers about their involvement, let alone the unofficial classified figures. I am not going to belabour the point by bringing in details about the Irangate scandal…the arms smuggled out and sold to both Iran and Iraq…the intervention in Lebanon…and the American troops landing on the Lebanese coast.'

Are this not victims of the continuous bombardment and shelling of the Palestinian camps in southern Lebanon during the 1967 occupation of the West Bank and Gaza Strip? I do not bring in details, they are common knowledge.'

At that moment Sarah's consultant shouted that he had found the papers, but Sarah said quietly that they were no longer needed.

The rebuttal by the prosecution was so impressive that the public rose in support, applauding. And the judge allowed it, waiting until the hubbub had died down and quiet settled again on the courtoom.

Sarah was asked if she had any more witnesses and she replied, 'In fact, Your Honour, I planned to bring another group from the south African victims of racial segregation which is backed by the superpowers. But I believe that enough is enough and I trust that the court appreciates the condition of the witnesses. I could bring them from Korea, the Philippines, South Sudan, Eritrea, Latin America, Nicaragua. Salvador. Argentina and elsewhere.

"These places have suffered because might and arms reign. Truth and justice and the search for peace have never been acknowledged. But only used as glittering slogans when political votes are needed.

'Might is right, your Honour. If not by nuclear weapons then by conventional weapons. Where these are not used, or where they fail, economic wars are used to bring about inflation, to ruin the economy of an adversary. The world economy may well be heading toward total collapse.

'Your Honour, we were hoping that our leaders would view the world more realistically, with a long-range outlook. With the prosecution's witnesses I hope that we have been able to convince the judicial council and jury that the sheer physical condition of the witnesses leaves no need for questions. Our ultimate goal in this trial is to demonstrate to everyone that the tragedies and suffering befalling the worlds and mankind stem from the power resting in the hands of leaders. Who, being human beings, cannot be trusted with the destructive means of war.

'Therefore the weapons must be destroyed. It is our wish that they had never been developed in the first place. I hope that the defence understands why these witnesses have been brought before you they are now at the disposal of the court'.

Sarah returned to her seat, tired mentally and physically. It was now the turn of the defence, who had been talking to the heads of state. Just as he had done to Sarah, the judge urged the defence counsel to speak. 'Gentlemen, do you wish to cross-examine the witnesses?'

'No!' replied their spokesman. 'We do not wish to, but as the prosecution did, the defence wishes to make a few comments. The prosecution's supposedly intelligent tactic, unprecedented in litigation procedures, of parading witnesses form various parts of the world, was meant to excite the emotions of the public and jury and to generate pressure from public opinion. But I remind my learned colleague of the inadvisability of such evidence in court. The court cannot be manipulated by these means'.

Here, Sarah's associate expressed his objection at the defence counsel's attempt to divert the course of the intention of the prosecution and the defence said '…if the court would allow me to finish my comments without interruption…'

The judge settled the quibbling 'Objection overruled!' he snapped. The defence was obviously happy by what seemed to be the winning of a point.

'As I was saying, the prosecution was trying to build up pressure from public opinion. But the court cannot be duped into admitting such a procedure. Nonetheless, the presiding judge, the judiciary council and the jury are human beings who can be influenced by these scenes of emotion-rousing witnesses, such is the objective of that parade'.

All the time the prosecution were making notes and it caught the attention of the defence counsel and he made a comment about it.

'Does the prosecution have any remarks to make about what I have just said? He asked, though there had been no objection to his words. Here, the judge broke in sharply. 'There has been no objection, so proceed!'

The defence made an error here by stopping and addressing the prosecution, who took the chance to recap what he had said about the court being occupied by human beings.

If they are human beings then they cannot be infallible. They are liable to make mistakes, to be put under psychological pressures. The judiciary and the leaders of the world share this quality, therefore the whole world is vulnerable, under human pressure, human frailty'.

The defence counsel realized that his own thoughts had reasserted the prosecution's claims, so he went on:

"The world would be in real jeopardy with so much weaponry in the charge of people. No matter how wise, balanced or learned they may be, they will always be vulnerable. Especially when challenges, competition, conflict, disagreement occur.

"the leaders here are human with the rest of humanity. It is not a *defect but a guarantee* of the continuation of the world. Mankind has been endowed with many capabilities unequalled by any other creature. Dread and fear *guarantee* peace-yeas, dread and fear!

'Allow me to go over the semantics of this quality'.

He went on to give a long speech on fear, ending, 'Our leaders had a fear concerning the destructive power of nuclear weapons, knowing their dangers. Consequently they took all precautionary measures against using them'.

These words did not ring true to some of the public. One of them rose to his feet in rage. He shouted, "Do you mean that they were developed and produced not for use but only for intimidation. Like the lions that used to be placed at the gates of ancient cities?'.

He judge banged his gavel loudly, then dropped it to the floor. both Sarah and the defence counsel went to pick it up and they reached for it together. Both wanted to grasp it and their eyes met. Who would give way? It was a symbol of the confrontation between prosecution and defence.

In a moment, Sarah felt the man's will was weakening and she pulled harder. It slipped from the man's hand and Sarah smiled, stood and handed it to the judge.

She said, 'the prosecution apologises on behalf of the gentleman who interrupted, we request the court's indulgence but at the same time adopt his question and objection!'

The judge called on the defence and informed him of the prosecution's position and the defence nodded. This took place before the bench and quietly the judge spoke to the court.

'I caution the people not to interrupt these proceedings. If anything of the sort happens again the perpetrator will be subject to penalty and removed. The prosecution has adopted the question and the defence has agreed to reply. Now let us proceed.'

But the defence counsel had been taken by surprise by this turn of events. He had herd the man shouting and had not expected Sarah or the court to take notice of it. Realising his difficulty he went back to his colleagues and after a moment he sat down and the other counsel rose.

This helped to salvage the situation and averted any embarrassment form his colleague. But he still wondered hoe to respond and repeated the man's question.

'Do you mean that they are developed and produced…who guarantees that?

"My first observation about this question', he went on, 'is that it was raised by a member of the public. This makes it inadmissible, but it shows that they are responsive and fully participating. However, if the prosecution had not adopted that question we would not need to address it.'

Some thought that the defence was playing for time in order to downgrade the importance of the question so that any reply would be accepted by the jury.

The counsel continued, 'Whoever asked the question seems to have missed the point of the previous statement about the psychological function of nuclear weapons, its using fear to prevent its use. It is a strategy known as 'mutual deterrence'. A kind of sabre rattling. It is something that all great powers have done through the ages. We cannot alter this on the basis of an objection in this case.

The prosecution rose and made a strong objection. 'Your honour, will the defence take note and not avoid our objective. We want to establish error and conviction. We are not the guarantors of change. This will be the job of the world when we have achieved our objective according tot he code of procedure of this court.'

The judge sustained the objection, emphasizing to the defence what the court was set up to achieve and what it was not concerned with. Again he reminded the defence of the terms of agreement. The defence accepted the ruling and continued.

'When this defence raises the issue of the mutual deterrence between the superpowers, he sees it as a preventative measure against the chances of mutual error. This can only achieved by the existence of equally strong powers, having equal capabilities. Otherwise there is an absence of balance. One power would rise to hegemony and domination over the world and this is where the danger lies.

'Nuclear weapons have taken their part in the world and no power has taken part in the arms race except to underline the continuation of balance.

'Your Honour, members of the jury, it must be clear to you without any further explanation that nuclear armament-or the race toward superiority and progress in that field is an ordinary, natural thing which is accepted in everyday life. The thesis that it is wrong must be proven. Making an accusation lodged against the leaders of the superpowers is unacceptable.

"To conclude this statement and to buttress it with evidence based on witness testimony, the defence will complete the questioning of the commander-in-chief of the first super military alliance. In turn, we also request questioning the commander of the opposing military alliance, the Warsaw Pact, which represents a bloc of countries posing a balance against the first alliance'.

The judge then called the leader of the Eastern bloc and a large man made way to the witness-box. That he was important was obvious from uniform and many medals. How was old but showed no sign of frailty and took the Oath as if he were being enlisted into an army.

Then he sat down.

He stated his name and rank, nationality, and added his qualifications. The first question came.

'Is he alliance still producing nuclear weapons and deploying them in other countries of the world?'

It was a question he had not expected, one about the policy of his alliance, but the counsel assured him that it was all known and there was no need to conceal anything.

He paused, trying to find a suitable beginning which showed shrewdness, even cunning, so that his answer would fit the court's context. He said, 'the alliance is following a policy that suits the nature of the present stage in history. Therefore heads of member states have agreed to curtail the production and proliferation of nuclear weapons. This policy is now in effect.'

'What do you mean by "the nature of the present stage" asked the defence.

And the witness's answer was that he meant the state of détente or rapprochement between the super-powers.

The next question was "have you reached an international concord guaranteeing peace and security in the world?'

He replied that the great role played by the leaders of the superpowers and other alliance members had produced a great deal of reconciliation imprinted in many treaties.

And that his state was in turn bond by their treaties.

'Do you foresee a nuclear attack from any country in the world?' asked the defence, to which the witness said that things were moving in the right direction in this connection. Judging by the accords and increasing understanding among the countries he did not foresee, at the moment, any aggression or nuclear hostile act from any country against another.

Suddenly there was a disturbance. The prosecution members were standing in a circle discussing a piece of paper held by a consultant. They seemed amused at the phrase 'At the present time'.

Perplexed, the witness did not see what the problem was.

Then he saw the look of disgust on the face of his defence colleague. He stifled the question, "what is all this about?'

The truth of the matter and the answer lay in the last part of his replly. It was an honest, candid answer, free from subtlety and finesse, yet, he not aware of its effect on the people in the court. The defence lawyer tried to amend things by putting another question.

'You are quite assured that there is nothing that could trigger a nuclear war between you and the countries of the other alliance?'

'None whatsoever!' the general replied.

'Then you are convinced that there is no need to fear?'

Now both Sarah and her consultant rose to object at the question on the grounds that it was conjecture and personal opinion.

The defence lawyer said, 'But this defence insists on it strongly, for it stands for an important opinion, though personal'.

Here, the judge had to stop the argument and allow the trial to proceed.

'Objection overruled! The question stands.'

Feeling that he had won a glorious victory the defence repeated the question.

The witness replied, 'Of course not! There was no need for this trial, which we never expected or foresaw.' And he added to himself 'we know what we have to do and we do not sit idle and wait for kids to teach us what to do!'

With these works the lawyer felt he had achieved what his questioning was supposed to do.

That he had reassured the jury, judiciary council, the public and the whole world that the issue before the court had been in safe hands and was the subject of international accords and treaties. On this basis he decided to stop and the prosecution their turn to cross-examine the witness, having finished his own questioning.

10

It was the turn of the prosecution. Sarah's assistant stood up, gathering his papers from the table and took the floor. He greeted the commander-in-chief of the military alliance, which pleased the man—his face showing signs of satisfaction and self-assurance in dealing with questions from a mere lad, assuming he was about to enjoy answering him.

Then the assistant following his greeting with a statement of the general's name, rank and a brief list of points about his military past. For example, he had participated in World War Two as a young soldier at the beginning of his military career. This was followed by some of the alliance's operations and periodic manoeuvres. He asked if the information were correct.

The general replied, 'Yes, but very brief. The details make several pages in the alliance's periodical publications.'

'True,' said the assistant. 'It was brief to save the court's time and in order not to burden you.' He spared no effort in trying to put his questions ands show respect for the old witness in order to make him feel at ease and establish a rapport. In so doing he soothed the anger engendered in himself by the defense counsel. The young assistant could sense the willing cooperation of the witness. Now he began his assault.

'Would you please give this court an idea about the reasons for forming this alliance and how many countries have joined it as members?'

'There is no doubt', said the general, 'that the world has passed through historical stages marked by wars and military confrontation between many countries. This has resulted in two great blocs with a deal of nearly parallel strength. These blocs represent the combined strength of the member countries brought together in an alliance for the next purpose of combating any danger or threat posed by any other party.'

The next question out to him was to ask if there was a good reason for countries to join the alliances.

The general nodded, 'Undoubtedly, the assemblage of the largest possible power, human or technological, leads to the formation of a super-power that has reckoned with in the world. It gives member countries the protection provided by the alliance in case of danger.'

'Do we assume, then,' said the assistant, 'that these countries were expecting some kind of danger. Or were apprehensive of some imminent threat which pushed them into the alliance?'

Again the general nodded. 'Yes and every country has its own evaluation of the dangers threatening it. For this reason we are committing to the alliance. Possibly the reason for drawing on the benefits of membership is in the form of protection through the alliance and aid from member states.'

Now, the young assistant was coming closer and closer to the real subject of the cross-examination. He asked another question. 'Therefore, if each state did not feel there was an imminent danger, it would not need to form a military and join the alliance?'

'Naturally!'

The assistant nodded, and asked, 'Is it possible for any state to foresee an imminent danger or aggression and to predict it's time and place?'

The general had the answer. 'Certainly, there are indications that forewarn of danger. Consequently, one can make predictions. As for it's time and place that is difficult. Each country or group tries to keep them secret. However, it is possible to make a guess from the thorough monitoring of military positions and movements.'

'So the whole matter is based on prediction?' asked the assistant, and the general nodded.

Then the prosecution hurled a direct question. 'The military preparedness of states and their memberships in alliances take place as contingency matters?'

'Why not? Yes?' said the general. The atmosphere had become tense and nerves highly strung. The defense was apprehensive as a potential trap set for the witness by the prosecution. He was being coaxed into something. The defense looked for an opportunity to object and break the prosecution's progress, but could see their way. And the witness could not see the connection between his answers.

The next question was, 'Can you justify the annual or seasonal manoeuvres and raining exercises held by the alliance?'

The general said, 'They held to ascertain the alliance's strength and to keep the forces of the alliance in a state of readiness and alertness.'

'Of course, "Readiness and alertness" for a possible aggression or attack?' said the prosecution.

'This is natural.'

The assistant asked then if the alliance tested or displayed all types of weaponry, and the general confirmed this, 'In manoeuvres or on separate occasions.'

'Including nuclear arms?'

'Yes!' relied the general as he sat up, pulling himself from his relaxed position as if preparing for a barrage of hostile questions.

The prosecution noticed the change in the witness's mental alertness at the mention of nuclear arms. But he chose to give him a break and allowed him to relax. He shuffled his papers about, then resumed as if introducing a new subject, with the general alert and ready to answer questions about nuclear arms.

Instead the prosecution asked, 'Considering that you were born in 1921, you were a young man at the outbreak of world war two and you participated out of your sense of duty to your country?'

Relaxed, the witness nodded.

'Did you at the time, as a citizen, expect the war to break out and hostilities to spread to the extent they did?'

'No. Nobody expected or even wanted to the war to break out. At the time, we considered the matter as one of political disagreement, while many people were warning of the eruption of war and were afraid of its expansion,' explained the general.

'Did you have any expectation of its length, expansion or what would happen?'

The witness shook his head at this, adding that to them it was something of the future, there was no way of predicting or ascertaining these things.

Now the prosecution wanted to pounce on the witness with questions that would destroy and invalidate his earlier statements and nullify their effects.

The next question was, 'How could you, then, answer in the negative the prosecution's question about the chances of nuclear war between the countries or alliances?'

Now the witness was sweating. He wiped his forehead. 'I do not recall saying that I ruled out the possibility of nuclear war!' he said.

The prosecution came back quickly. 'It was implied in your answer to a question from the defense. We would have objected but we thought it more convenient to leave for comment until this moment.'

'Let us be more honest, more specific. You did not say, "I did not expect". But you exactly said...' he raised his notes '...you said, "Sir, you are confident there was nothing to cause a nuclear war between you and the countries of the other alliance".'

As he heard the prosecution read the question and his reply to it, the general relaxed from his tenseness and sighed as if with relief.

"None whatsoever, I'm sure!" that was you answer.'

What had caused the change from tenseness to relaxation? In fact, the witness had proved the explanation implicitly in the explanation of his intention, when he gave the answer earlier in his testimony. There was no contradiction in what he said. That was how he got himself out of that corner.

He explained, 'I said there was no worry of nuclear war. Yes, at least at present. And this, as I remember, was the point of the question.'

The prosecution came back, 'Yes, sir. You are correct. The defense asked the question about the present time and your answer was truly related to the absence of worry about a possible nuclear war now. But can you vouch for it not to break out in the future?'

The witness retorted, 'But who can vouch for the future?'

'Can anyone do that, even though all countries were opposed to it?' asked the prosecution.

The general hesitated. He tried to give a clear answer. 'But there are pacts and treaties, and…'

The prosecution abruptly broke in, 'There is no need for this kind of answer. We want a definite answer from your own experience, an honest answer.'

Now the defense wanted to put up a strong objection and stood up, but the judge intervened, stopping it and motioning him to sit down. The atmosphere was tense throughout the courtroom. Everyone was waiting to hear the word they knew already. But they wanted to hear it from a man in a responsible position, with experience of the subject. The monitor cameras were scanning the scene, moving round so as not to miss anything.

The prosecution repeated the question for the witness, who was very uncomfortable. He burst out, 'No one can guarantee the prevention of a nuclear or any other war!'

Silence engulfed the court, the entire base. The man lowered his head, trying to pull himself together and put his thoughts in order. And the prosecution gave him the chance, waiting for him, waiting in anticipation.

Then he began talking without being asked, in fact he started putting questions to the prosecution. 'Do you, young man who has been taught how to conduct a court trial, guarantee the prevention of any aggression against us from any party?'

Everyone felt that there was a change in the tone of the question toward sincerity and truth; the courtroom was surprised by this new honest attitude. No one could hide anything any more.

Sarah and her associates sensed that they had to show the witness as well as all those present the kind of respect due to parents. The prosecution had inflicted suffering and fatigue upon him by disclosing the plans of the alliance. But they were not revealing a crime that had not been committed in premeditation. What they did was uncover a fatal error facing the entire world due consideration.

The witness seemed to be weak and unable to rise and get to the witness box to answer the questions. Sarah and her assistant helped him while the question was repeated, 'Can you guarantee that?'

There seemed to be a father-child relationship building up between them, unspoiled by conflict but marked by tender feelings.

Sarah said, 'We cannot, we don't guarantee the absence of aggression by any group against any other. It is in the hands of people and in human nature. But we, exactly like you, are looking for the guarantee. We hope to find a motive that will force the world to rid itself of nuclear weapons before the time comes when they are used to wipe us all out.'

The old man spoke again, 'You are just like us! You are today's generation looking for a guarantee. We ask, "Who can give such a guarantee"?'

At this moment the trial had moved people to despondency about humanity which covered the entire base.

At the same moment they were totally amazed, for the door of the hall swung open noisily. As the door slowly opened all the people quietly turned to see. It was as if the heavy door was being pushed by someone who did not have the strength.

Then as a gap appeared in the doorway, two hands appeared carrying a bundle wrapped in white, followed by a body. It was a man pushing against the weight of the door with his body. He had been trying to get in and heard the argument about the guarantee. As he at last got through the gap a security guard rushed to help him.

It was a young man in his thirties who could hardly walk unaided but he refused the offers of help. The package seemed to be so heavy that it was dragging him down and he swayed from side to side.

At last, he managed to approach the bench and shouted, 'This is the guarantee! Here it is!'

People stood to watch as he passed and repeated it, 'This is the guarantee!'

It was what everyone had been waiting for. Since he seemed to be carrying the guarantee he was shown a great deal of respect. He approached the partition separated the public from the defense and the prosecution, still repeating the words.

Because of his injuries, there were only signs of good looks and a kind nature. He stumbled several times, but by the time he reached the bench everyone was standing.

He said again, 'Here is your guarantee. It is the future generation in the name of God. In the name of mankind and humanity. In the name of compassion. In the name of goodness. Please put an end to destruction and annihilating weaponry before you perish with them.'

His speech was difficult to understand but they could see the reason for his disability. His words held everyone's attention.

'I, David, present my son to you as a symbol of the future generation. He is the offspring of his mother Mary and myself. She delivered him into the world before giving up her soul and her body as a sacrifice for convening this court.'

Sarah was dumbfounded by the sight, even her thinking had been paralyzed. She had recognised him and had shouted, 'David!'. As she tried to go to him she collapsed. Security guards rushed forward, calling for a doctor.

But David was not stopped by the sight of Sarah unconscious on the floor of the courtroom. His concentration was directed towards his mission. He stood, swaying, and spoke again.

'Mary, my wife, passed away in suffering while struggling to assemble this court in which we all are. I am part of the reason. When she saw my disfigured body, she vowed to do something to rid the world of war and the means of the destruction of mankind.'

'I hope you reached a common point of agreement for which my son is the guarantee. For the sake of tomorrow's generation-they are our future-for guaranteeing a decent life free from threats, danger, destruction and terror, I leave my son as the witness for your decision and verdict. His generation will have their judgement on this trial.'

He left his son on the bench and walked toward the door. He passed through it and was soon out of sight. The door was closed behind him.

Why did they continue to stare at the closed door? It was not clear. Perhaps they were expecting another surprise to come through that door? Did they imagine a picture imprinted on the door showing all the previous events, a sight that told the world it was separated from its demise by nothing but a straw.

That last straw which could be too much for this world.

0-595-32309-X